START A SUCCESSFUL BUSINESS IN OREGON

Douglas L. Clark

Self-Counsel Press Inc.
a subsidiary of
International Self-Counsel Press Ltd.
Head and Editorial Office
Vancouver, British Columbia
U.S. Warehouse
Seattle, Washington

Copyright 1977 in Canada by Self-Counsel Press Inc.

All rights reserved. No part of this book may be reproduced or transmitted in any form by any means without permission in writing from the publisher, except by a reviewer, who may quote brief passages in a review.

ISBN 0 - 88908 - 803 - 9

Printed in Canada

First edition: June, 1977

Self-Counsel Press Inc.
1303 N. Northgate Way
Seattle, Washington 98133
a subsidiary of
International Self-Counsel Press Ltd.
Head and Editorial Office
306 West 25th Street
North Vancouver
British Columbia, Canada V7N 2G1
Telephone: (604) 986-3366
Warehouses in
Seattle Victoria Vancouver Calgary Winnipeg Toronto

CONTENTS

FOREWORD

1 **WHO CAN BECOME THEIR OWN BOSS?**   1
- a. Why run your own business?   1
- b. Lack of money is no obstacle   2
- c. Don't worry about security   2
- d. Utilize your special talents   2
- e. You make the rules   3

2 **SETTING YOUR GOALS**   5
- a. Money   5
- b. Money vs. your personal life   5
- c. Attaining your financial goal   6

3 **WHAT KIND OF BUSINESS?**   8
- a. What are your skills and interests?   8
- b. What retail and service businesses are needed in your area?   8
- c. What resources are near you?   10
- d. What is unique in your community?   10
- e. What services do your local industries need?   10
- f. Are there any federal installations nearby?   11
- g. What is unique to Oregon?   13
- h. What is new or in keeping with the times?   14
- i. Take a tip from the experts   14
- j. Is your community growing?   16
- k. What about wood products?   17

4 **WHERE TO LOCATE**   19
- a. Retail and service businesses   19
- b. Manufacturing and wholesale operations   23
- c. Tourist recreation businesses   29

5	**OPERATING A BUSINESS FROM YOUR HOME**	32
	a. Rented premises	33
	b. Operating at home	34
	c. When not to use your home	36

6	**HOW TO GET STARTED**	38
	a. Following the rules and regulations	38
	b. What kind of business organization?	39
	c. Forming a corporation	41
	d. The sale of securities	43
	e. Authorization for out-of-state corporations to transact business in Oregon	44
	f. State and federal requirements	45

7	**HOW TO GET FINANCING**	66
	a. Be practical and realistic	68
	b. Making a good impression	70
	c. Have a prepared plan on paper	71

8	**WHERE TO GET FINANCING**	76
	a. Banks	76
	b. Personal sources	80
	c. What about selling some of the equity?	80
	d. Equity capital sources here in the Northwest	84
	e. Federal sources	89
	f. Factoring	91
	g. Insurance companies	92
	h. Pension funds	93
	i. Investment brokers	93
	j. Equipment-leasing companies	94
	k. Port districts	94
	l. Other sources of funds	95

9	**WHAT TO DO WHEN YOU ARE SHORT OR CASH**	97
	a. Have supplies bill you on your best day	98
	b. Use discount day payment	98
	c. Refinance fixed obligations	99

	d.	Spread out major purchases	99
	e.	Make every day a billing day	100
	f.	Plug the loopholes	100
	g.	Keep aware of past due accounts	101
	h.	Cut off the deadbeats	102
10	**TAXES**	103
	a.	Federal taxes	104
	b.	Oregon state taxes	106
	c.	Local taxes	107
11	**ORGANIZING TO PAY THE LOWEST TAXES POSSIBLE**	109
	a.	Sole proprietorships	109
	b.	Partnerships	110
	c.	Corporations	112
12	**OPERATING TO PAY THE LOWEST TAXES POSSIBLE**	116
	a.	How to lower your taxable income	116
	b.	Using your home for your business	117
	c.	Using your automobile in the business	118
	d.	Business entertainment	119
	e.	Maintenance and repairs	119
	f.	Office expenses, postage, and stationery	120
	g.	Medical and dental expenses	120
	h.	Tax payments	121
	i.	Self-employed retirement plans	121
13	**WHAT ABOUT BUYING A BUSINESS?**	122
	a.	Why buy a business?	122
	b.	Locating and purchasing a business	123
	c.	Financing the transaction	127
	d.	Conclusion	128
14	**WHAT ABOUT FRANCHISING?**	129
	a.	Introduction	129
	b.	What is franchising?	130

		c.	The franchise contract	131
		d.	Advantages and disadvantages	132
		e.	How franchisees are chosen	134
		f.	Finding the right franchise	134
		g.	What do you require from a franchise?	136

15 THE INS AND OUTS OF IMPORT/EXPORT BUSINESS — 137
a. Where to start — 137
b. Exporting — 139
c. Importing — 142

16 MANGING EMPLOYEES — 146
a. Motivate — 147
b. Compensation — 150
c. Handling creative people — 150

17 MORE SUCCESS TIPS — 152
a. Review your money goal — 152
b. Never stop learning — 152
c. Your competition can help — 153
d. Make your own decisions — 154
e. Use time effectively — 155
f. Establish a work schedule — 155
g. Plan leisure time — 156
h. Keep expenses down — 156
i. If you want something — ask for it — 157
j. Make friends with people like yourself — 157
k. Get free advertising through news releases — 158
l. Does the weather affect your business? — 159
m. Business protection insurance — 160
n. Management counselling — 162

APPENDIX — 163

BIBLIOGRAPHY — 164

LIST OF SAMPLES

1	Business Plan	72
2	Projected Operating Statement	75

FOREWORD

Why did you decide to open this particular book? No doubt you've had a dream about running your own business for years. It may only be a fleeting daydream that comes once in a blue moon or when the boss gives you a hard time. Maybe you have it refined to the point where you even know what kind of business you'd like it to be. Yet, somehow you've never dared to take the big jump. Well, maybe you're ready to start. Of course, *anyone* can start. The trick is to make a *success* of it!

   Once, I was also strictly a company man, but I left a successful 20-year career in engineering to set up my own consulting engineering practice. Along the way, I got involved in industrial development work, assisting others to get started in business. So, I know, from personal experience, that you can start a successful business right here in the Northwest.

   This book contains a mixture of success tips and hard factual research. I've seen these techniques used many times, and they really do work! Follow them, and you, too, can be on the road to success.

1
WHO CAN BECOME THEIR OWN BOSS?

a. WHY RUN YOUR OWN BUSINESS?
There are many reasons for going into business for yourself, but the main ones are probably:
- (a) To achieve personal independence
- (b) To develop your own ideas
- (c) To create a job for yourself, when nothing else is available
- (d) To earn a better income
- (e) To do what you want to do

Notice that I have specifically excluded such things as: escaping an unhappy work situation, having an easier job, or just being a boss.

If you choose to be your own boss for the last three reasons, your chances of success are going to be pretty slim. No one should go into business thinking it's going to be easy. You must be aware of the hazards involved, and think of how to avoid them beforehand.

One of the biggest difficulties is that you must train yourself to think of profits all the time. Otherwise, why bother going into business for yourself? Even more important, if you don't worry about them, no one else will either — except your family. (We'll talk more about that later.)

b. LACK OF MONEY IS NO OBSTACLE
Are you worried about capital? Don't be! The right idea, service, or product is what you should be thinking about. Once you have discovered what you have to offer and thought of a way to sell it (continually, to a growing list of clients), you can raise the capital to get started almost

anywhere. Later in this book, I will show you how to put together a proposal for a lender or investor, which will help you to put your best foot forward. With a little ingenuity, you can cut your initial needs down to a manageable amount. When you've arrived at that stage and have put together a good business plan, you will find that money is available.

Thousands of ordinary people — just like you and me — have started their own businesses on practically pennies. Why not you? Remember! The less you borrow or invest, the less you have to pay back. The rest is profit.

c. DON'T WORRY ABOUT SECURITY

"But what about security?" you may ask. That's really a very fleeting thing. Even the biggest companies hit bad times now and then, and have to lay off thousands of employees. So, where's the security in working for a big company? When you look at it, the only security you and I have are the abilities we were born with: our skills, ideas, common sense, and ingenuity. Only by using them to their fullest, and keeping them from getting rusty do we gain a richer life and a greater degree of security. Not by working a dull eight to five job for a cranky boss, and a wage that never quite keeps up with inflation! That's not security, that's drudgery!

d. UTILIZE YOUR SPECIAL TALENTS

Make a list of your particular goals and objectives in life, then of your skills and talents, and finally, of your job experience. Be specific. Don't just list "mechanically inclined." Instead, list "can repair bicycles," "can repair small appliances," "trained to repair automatic transmissions," "experienced in minor tune-up work."

By doing this, you will discover some combination of abilities and interests you have already that you could merge into a full-time business.

For example, a former air force pilot and glider enthusiast, was working in a warehouse. It bored him and the pay was poor. Finally, he thought carefully about his situation, quit his job, formed a gliding club, charged reasonable membership fees and instruction rates, and is now rich, happy, and doing what he loves. Now, he even designs and builds personalized gliders — and makes lots of money doing it!

Can you see how doing what you like best can pay off in profits?

Here's another example. A navy officer was ruled unfit for further service after an injury, but just couldn't forget the sea. Instead of crying in his beer, he bought, on a low-payment plan, a used fishing boat and runs his own pleasure-fishing charter service. He's happy as his own boss and growing steadily richer. (That's what I mean by turning your hobby or first love into a professional business.)

Incidentally, if this example happens to appeal to you or if any business where you need a commercially-sized boat is your dream, here's a money-saving tip. Due to the so-called Judge Boldt decision, the state of Washington is buying out many of the commercial fishing boats in that state. These are being auctioned off every few months at a fraction of their normal cost. The only restriction is that they can never again be used for commercial fishing in the state of Washington or the Columbia River. Oregon residents are in an excellent position to take advantage of this unusual opportunity. For details contact the Washington Department of Fisheries, Olympia, Washington.

e. YOU MAKE THE RULES

However, before you are convinced, let me give you one warning. In order to enjoy the fruits of independence and profits by running your own business, you must have self-discipline.

By that I mean you must be a tough boss and make yourself do the things that bring success. Does this sound rough? Not really. If you work for someone else, they make the rules. If you work for yourself, you make the rules — rules that are more in keeping with your personal desires and life needs.

Now, I started this chapter by asking: "Who can become their own boss?" The answer is: "You can," if you set your mind to being a successful business owner. But no one is asking *you* to spend 24 hours a day at the job.

2
SETTING YOUR GOALS

a. MONEY

Your only reason for starting your own business, in the first place, is to be your own boss and to make a certain amount of money. Your "search for wealth" must be a big thing in your life. You must have faith in yourself and your money-making plans.

Let's dispel any misgivings about making money. Making money is not a mysterious, awesome secret meant only for a chosen few. Far from it. Actually, making money is just about the easiest thing to do in this world — provided you have a money goal, skills, know-how, and drive to get what you want out of life.

Simple formula, isn't it? It is somewhat harder to put into practice, however, for in order to reach your money goal, you must have motivation, know-how, and a workable money plan with a time limit! Nevertheless, there is no reason why you cannot obtain *economic independence* which, in turn, will give you the personal independence to do what you want to do. What more could you really want?

b. MONEY vs. YOUR PERSONAL LIFE

"But," you argue, "some successful business people are millionaires many times over, yet seem to devote 24 hours a day to work. Really, they cannot enjoy that kind of grind day in and day out — or can they?" The truth is, of course, that they truly do enjoy their work, and the money is strictly a way of keeping score. (See what can happen when you work at something you like?)

Now, perhaps this way of living is not to your liking, and there is no doubt that these people sacrifice other things in life, such as family and friends. But no one is asking *you* to spend 24 hours a day at the job.

Speaking personally, I've had the great satisfaction of designing and building several multi-million dollar plants. During those years, I became so wrapped up in these projects that I worked many, many long days, weekends, and took few vacations. Despite that, I look back on those days as some of the happiest of my life. But I began to realize that my wife and family were getting short-changed in the deal.

Now, I try to balance the needs of my work with the needs of my family. That's one of the reasons why I'm back in Oregon. This is where we can relax and enjoy life, while at the same time, I'm building a new business career.

I am sure we all know or have heard of some very rich business people who devote their whole lives to making money and are millionaires because of it but have no home or family life. To me, this is the very reason for being in business — so that you have the time and money to enjoy the people and things you love.

c. ATTAINING YOUR FINANCIAL GOAL

You should write down the money goal (say, per month) that you would like to attain at the end of a five-year period when your business is firmly established and you can afford to relax a bit.

Next, list the amount of money that you need just to get by. Be ruthless in listing only those things that are unavoidable expenses. After that, go through the list and see which one of those you can cut without causing undue hardship.

For example, say your car is costing $100 a month for gas, maintenance, and insurance. Do you need that big a car? Do you fill up at discount stations? Can you do some of your own repairs? If not, do you have a mechanic friend who could do the repairs in exchange for something you can do?

Here is another example. You own a house and are paying off a rather large mortgage. Do you know that, by using part of the house for business purposes, you can write off part of those mortgage payments, not to mention part of the taxes, maintenance, and utilities payments?

Trivial you say? Not so. If you are paying off a mortgage now costing, say, $300 per month (most of which is interest) plus taxes, maintenance, and utilities of another $150 per month, for a total outlay of $450, you actually need to earn about $650 at today's tax rates to have that $450! By using, say, one-third of the house for business purposes, for storage, or for an office, you can write off approximately $150 per month, which saves you $50 per month in taxes. That's $600 per year (almost enough for a vacation). (This is discussed in chapter 10 on taxes.)

These are only a couple of examples. You would be amazed at the savings that can result from a little critical analysis of your spending habits.

"But," you say, "I'm not going into business to scrimp and save." That's not the point. The purpose of this whole exercise is to determine for yourself what you need to live on, while establishing your business. By doing this, and adding on your other business costs — goods, advertising, other people's wages, rent, and so on — you can easily determine your break-even point or, in simpler terms, what you need to sell on a month-by-month basis to make it. Anyway, even if your income is temporarily cut back, you have attained something that is priceless in the exchange — personal independence.

Here knowledge enters your money-goal picture. You must learn how to attract money to you. You must do the thing you love doing most of all, in a professional manner, in order to get that X number of dollars you want by a certain date.

3

WHAT KIND OF BUSINESS?

Earlier, I mentioned that you should analyze your skills and experience to decide what type of business to go into. If that didn't give you any clear direction, don't be discouraged. There are literally thousands of very successful businesses in this country that require only a basic education and just good common sense to operate.

Whether or not you've already decided on a type of business, let's look at some of the possibilities.

a. WHAT ARE YOUR SKILLS AND INTERESTS?

Obviously, you've got to be interested in whatever business you choose, or you're not going to enjoy operating it. Those skills that you've developed over the years are more than likely the things you've enjoyed doing. Most mechanics that I have met have always loved tinkering with cars from the time they first learned what a wrench was. The main thing to remember is that you are going to eat, sleep, and breathe this business. So, pick something you like.

Look at your hobbies. I've personally known several avid photography fans who have turned what was once a hobby into thriving photography businesses. Does anyone know a stamp dealer that didn't start out as a stamp collector? How many sporting goods shops are operated by someone who hasn't been a sports enthusiast all his life?

b. WHAT RETAIL AND SERVICE BUSINESSES ARE NEEDED IN YOUR AREA?

In the next chapter, we'll talk about where to locate a business. It's an important decision that can have a significant effect on the success of your business. But, you may have strong personal reasons for locating a business right where you live, or in some other community you particularly like. That's fine, but it means that you need to analyze what's already there to decide what else could go there. The Small Business Administration has published data on the average number of inhabitants in a particular market area for various types of businesses. It is included here for your careful study.

AVERAGE NUMBER OF INHABITANTS PER STORE BY TYPE OF BUSINESS

Type of Business	Inhabitants	Type of Business	Inhabitants
Grocery stores	1,534	Lumber and building material	8,124
Meat and fish markets	17,876	Paint, glass, wallpaper	22,454
Confectionery stores	31,409	Hardware stores	10,206
Retail bakeries	12,563	Farm equipment dealers	14,793
Dairy product stores	41,587	Auto dealers, new and used	6,000
Restaurants, lunchrooms	1,583	Auto dealers, used only	17,160
Cafeterias	19,341	Tire, battery, accessory dealers	8,764
Refreshment places	3,622	Boat dealers	61,526
Taverns, cocktail lounges	2,414	Household trailer dealers	44,746
Variety stores	10,373	Service stations	1,195
General merchandise stores	9,837	Antique and second-hand stores	17,169
Women's clothing stores	7,102	Book and stationery stores	28,584
Women's accessories stores	25,824	Drug stores	4,268
Men's and boys' clothing stores	11,832	Florists	13,531
Family clothing stores	16,890	Fuel oil dealers	25,425
Shoe stores	9,350	Garden supply stores	65,118
Furniture stores	7,210	Gift, souvenir shops	26,313
Floor covering stores	29,543	Feed and grain stores	16,978
Drapery, curtain upholstery stores	62,460	Hobby, toy, game shops	61,430
Houshold appliance stores	12,585	Jewelry stores	13,495
Radio and TV stores	20,346	Mail-order houses	44,067
Record shops	112,144	Optical goods stores	62,878
Musical instrument stores	46,332	Sporting goods stores	27,063

Source: *Starting and Managing a Small Business of Your Own*, 3rd ed. Small Business Administration, 1973.

This data should help you to decide whether or not your community could support the particular business you have in mind. For instance, in my community there are 40 grocery stores. If each store needs 1,534 people to support it, then we have a pretty good balance, because there are about 60,000 people in the immediate area. So, you might not consider my community as a very good place to locate another grocery store. On the other hand, it is also one of the fastest growing areas in the state. Probably, 1,534 people will move into the area within the next year. So, there will be room for one more grocery fairly soon.

CAUTION! These figures are national averages. They must be used with discretion in analyzing any given area. For example, Pendleton and Klamath Falls have basically the same populations. Being in a major agricultural area, Pendleton obviously needs more feed and grain stores than Klamath Falls. On the other hand, Klamath Falls probably needs more boat dealers than Pendleton.

Another way to analyze this problem is to compare the Yellow Pages of the telephone book in your community with those in a similar-sized community elsewhere. What businesses do they have that yours doesn't? Ask yourself: "Why?" Do this for several cities. You may turn up some interesting ideas.

c. WHAT RESOURCES ARE NEAR YOU?

Do you live by the ocean or on the Columbia River? These areas could support many types of marine-related businesses, such as fishing, aquaculture, marine transportation, and boat repair. Eastern Oregon, on the other hand, can support irrigation supply dealers, pesticide application operators, and well drillers. Look over your area. Is there a big deposit of sand or gravel nearby? Maybe you could start a quarry.

d. WHAT IS UNIQUE TO YOUR COMMUNITY?

Are you sitting in the middle of a tourists' paradise? Then consider a motel, travel trailer park, restaurant, souveir shop, or some form of entertainment for them.

Is your community one of the original settlements in this part of the country? If historically-minded people are visiting your community on a regular basis, maybe an antique store would do well. Maybe you could capitalize on an old-fashioned theme, like a gay 90's ice-cream parlor.

Does your community have a special theme? You've probably heard of the great success Leavenworth, Washington has enjoyed since adopting a Bavarian alpine village motif. This sort of theme lends itself to all sorts of specialized stores capitalizing on that idea — clothing stores selling Bavarian costumes, delicatessens selling special imported German foods, and restaurants featuring Bavarian dishes. Now, I know that there aren't too many Leavenworths around. However, the same idea can be used on a neighborhood level. I suspect that there are a number of ethnic settlements around the state. If you live in or near one of these, do a little research on what unique businesses the "old" country has that we don't see very often around here.

e. WHAT SERVICES DO YOUR LOCAL INDUSTRIES NEED?

Do you live in a city with a heavy concentration and variety of industries? Then get to know the purchasing agents for these firms. Find out where they purchase all their supplies and services. A wide variety of industrial machinery and equipment have some very basic items in common that require continual repair and replacement — bearings, V-belts, gears, and so on. A local supply for these types of items could be very helpful. Similarly, there are some very basic services any industry can use, like welding shops and machine shops. Any type of maintenance service is welcome in an industrial area because it is an activity that has many ups and downs in work load. Few industries try to staff their maintenance departments for peak demands.

f. ARE THERE ANY FEDERAL INSTALLATIONS NEARBY?

All federal agencies operate under rules which require that a certain percentage of their procurements be placed with small businesses. Check around and see what supplies and services they need. Each location should have a person specifically assigned to procure supplies from small businesses. In Oregon you should contact these people:

Mr. John Boyd
Umatilla Army Depot
Hermiston, Oregon 97838

Mrs. Virginia A. Brower
827 Air Defense Group
Kingsley Field
Klamath Falls, Oregon 97601

Mr. Frederick A. Krebs
U.S. Army Engineer District
P.O. Box 2946
Portland, Oregon 97205

Mr. Earl Redding
U.S. Army Engineer Division
North Pacific
210 Customs House
Portland, Oregon 97209

Mr. Karl T. Lehmann
Wood Products Office
DCSC Defense Supply Administration
2850 S.E. 82nd Avenue
Portland, Oregon 97266

Regional Director of Business Affairs
General Services Administration
440 Federal Building
915 Second Avenue
Seattle, Washington 98174

Mr. Herb McCleary
Department of the Interior
Bonneville Power Administration
P.O. Box 3621
Portland, Oregon 97208

Mr. Robert Crowe
Department of Agriculture
U.S. Forest Service — Region 6
P.O. Box 3623
Portland, Oregon 97208

Mr. Richard Mundinger
Department of the Interior
Fish & Wildlife Service
P.O. Box 3737
1500 N.E. Irving Street
Portland, Oregon 97208

Mr. E. LaCourse
Department of the Interior
Bureau of Indian Affairs
P.O. Box 3785
1425 N.E. Irving Street
Portland, Oregon 97208

Prime contractors to various federal agencies also operate under similar rules to the agencies themselves. If you have any firms in this category in your area, contact the purchasing agent for details on their small business procurement program.

g. WHAT IS UNIQUE TO OREGON?

For a long time we on the West Coast had an inferiority complex about our location. People would mean, "Oh, we're too far removed from the main markets in this country to ever do very well." Well, the picture has changed dramatically in the past decade. Instead of saying we're too far removed from the 200 million population market in the United States people are now realizing that we are actually strategically located to serve the billion-plus population market that is located on the whole North Pacific Rim, including Japan, China, Korea, and Russia. And take a look at that awakening giant, Alaska.

What does all this mean to Oregon! Well, for one thing, it means that this is an excellent place to go into the import/export business. Just take a look at the increase in foreign trade through the Columbia River ports during the past 10 years.

FOREIGN TRADE THROUGH PORTLAND DISTRICT PORTS
(Short Tons)

Year	Imports	Exports
1966	1,942,476	7,854,082
1968	2,247,195	9,130,413
1970	2,878,911	10,371,501
1972	3,239,109	10,729,539
1974	4,244,772	13,611,300

Source: U.S. Army Corps of Engineers, *Waterborne Commerce of the United States, 1975*, Part IV, (San Francisco [Washington, D.C.: Government Printing Office, 1976 (?)]), p. 40.

The Oregon State Department of Transportation estimated that the total economic impact of all this activity to the state of Oregon was $678,004,000 in 1971. Care to tap into this goldmine? (In chapter 9 I will tell you how to get into the import/export business.)

h. WHAT IS NEW OR IN KEEPING WITH THE TIMES?

We are in a time of rapid change. This opens up great opportunities for newcomers who are able to spot the trends and take quick action to capitalize on them. With the energy crisis still unresolved, there are increasingly important energy conservation products to be manufactured, sold, and installed. Also, look at the nostalgia trend. It seems as though more and more items from the "good old days" are coming back.

i. TAKE A TIP FROM THE EXPERTS

When thinking about a new business, it is a good idea to check up on what the experts predict for the future of the particular type of product you are planning to make or sell. These experts come in many guises. It may be the business editor of your local newspaper commenting on the future outlook of some facet of local commerce; it may be a local business leader speaking before the local Chamber of Commerce; it may be an economist for the state or a large bank writing an annual economic report for the area you live in; or it could be a long-range outlook prepared by some state, federal, or business association.

A particularly interesting report was recently issued by the U.S. Department of Commerce. It goes into quite a bit of detail in making projections on the growth of a wide variety of industries over the next 10 years. The following table shows the amount of growth in sales they predict for some of the more rapidly growing industries. So here's your chance to "hitch your wagon to a shooting star." Just a word of caution though. Always take such predictions with a grain of salt; even the experts get fooled now and then.

GROWTH PROJECTIONS TO 1985

Industry	1975 Sales $ Billion	1985 Forecast $ Billion
Mobile Homes	2.0	9.0
Commercial Lighting Fixtures	2.6	6.5
Motor Vehicles and Equipment	38.0	83.0
Fiber Boxes	6.3	15.8
Folding Paper Boxes	1.8	3.5
Food Products	176.0	393.0
Alcoholic Beverages	9.0	20.0
Soft Drinks	7.0	20.7
Household Appliances	7.9	16.5
Furniture	7.9	17.8
Jewelry	2.1	4.6
Toys, Games, Children's Vehicles	2.4	4.7
Sporting Goods	1.9	3.9
Photographic Equipment and Supplies	7.6	14.7
Electronic Equipment	25.5	52.7
Computers and Calculators	10.5	22.6
Cable Television	0.7	3.0
General Industrial Machinery	16.8	42.7
Material Handling Equipment	3.7	10.3
Farm Equipment	6.5	16.6
Construction Equipment	8.9	21.0
Food Production Machinery	1.7	4.1
Engineering and Scientific Instruments	1.5	4.3
Automatic Environmental Controls	0.7	2.0
Measuring and Control Equipment	2.4	6.7

Source: U.S. Department of Commerce, Domestic and International Business Adminsitration, *U.S. Industrial Outlook 1976: With Projections to 1985* (Washington, D.C.: Government Printing Office, 1976).

j. IS YOUR COMMUNITY GROWING?

If you live in a growing community, you obviously have many opportunities for starting a business that would not exist in a static community. Probably one of the more obvious opportunities is in home construction. More people mean more homes. Already I can hear you saying: "Yes, that's great for carpenters, but I'm no carpenter." Well, my answer to you is this: "You're forgetting this is the age of specialization! You don't need to be a carpenter to carve out your share of a housing boom."

Just to give you an idea, here is a list of specialties in the construction field. Any one or a combination of several can be the basis for a successful contracting business.

Air conditioning
Acoustical work
Antenna installation
Awning installation
Asphalt paving
Boiler erection
Burglar alarm installation
Bricklaying
Blasting
Breakwater construction
Bridge construction
Bowling alley installation
Cesspool construction
Communication equipment
Chimney construction
Carpentry
Coppersmithing
Concrete construction
Culvert installation
Concrete reinforcement
Cable laying
Caisson drilling
Calking
Carpetlaying
Core drilling
Door and window installation
Dam construction
Dock construction
Drainage
Dredging
Dampproofing
Dismantling
Demolition
Dry wall construction
Electrical
Earthmoving
Fuel oil burner installation
Fire alarm installation
Fresco work
Fence construction
Fireproofing
Garage door installation
Gutter and downspout
Gunniting
General contracting
Grading
Heating equipment
Hardwood flooring
Insulation installation
Lathing
Linoleum laying
Leadburning
Lighting installation
Mechanical
Marble work
Masonry
Mosaic work
Mastic flooring
Metal ceiling installation
Metal building front

Manhole construction
Plumbing
Painting
Paperhanging
Plastering
Posthole digging
Pile driving
Pipe laying
Paint and wallpaper stripping
Power generating equipment
Refrigeration
Retaining wall construction
Roofing work
Railroad construction
Refractory installation
Septic tank installation
Sheetmetal work
Sprinkler systems
Sump pump installation
Sound systems
Skylight installation

Sidewalk and curb construction
Stucco work
Surfacing concrete floors
Sewer construction
Soil compaction
Scaffolding work
Stonesetting
Sheetrock taping
Shoring and underpinning
Telephone installation
Terrazo work
Tile installation
Tinsmithing
Trenching
Underground utilities
Ventilation
Weatherstripping
Welding
Window shade/venetian blinds
Water well drilling

k. WHAT ABOUT WOOD PRODUCTS?

I would be remiss if I didn't point out some of the possibilities for utilizing wood as the basic raw material for a small manufacturing operation. After all, Oregon is one of the major producers of timber products in the country. Why not capitalize on an abundant low-cost raw material as the basis of your business? Here's a list of products that can be made from wood. Maybe one or several can be your key to fortune.

Awnings
Arches, laminated
Beds
Bookcases
Buffets
Beauty bark
Barrel heading and staves
Benches
Boxes
Baskets
Beekeeping supplies
Bowls
Bungs
Cants, resawed lumber
Cutstock

Cabinets
Chests
Crates
Clothes driers
Clothespins
Curtain stretchers
Coat racks
Croquet sets
Chairs
Coffee tables
Cots
Cradles
Cribs
Costumers
Dimension lumber

Doors and trim
Drums
Dishes
Display racks
Dowels
Desks
Dressers
Dressing tables
Excelsior
End tables
Fence rails
Furniture stock
Frames for box springs
Filing cabinets
Flats
Gun stocks
Garage doors
Garment hangers
Garden furniture
Headboards
High chairs
Handles
Hampers
Kegs
Ladders
Letters and numbers
Locks
Matchsticks
Moldings
Meat hammers
Mallets
Magazine racks
Oars
Ornamental woodwork
Piling
Poles
Posts
Pickets
Parquet flooring
Prefabricated buildings
Pails
Pressing blocks
Picture frames
Paint sticks
Pallets
Pencil slats
Pressed sawdust logs
Pulleys

Play pens
Partitions
Pedestals
Railroad ties
Roof trusses
Reals
Rollers
Rolling pins
Rulers and yardsticks
(better yet, metersticks —
everyone will need one soon)
Rockers
Scaffolds
Scoops
Shoe trees
Signboards
Spools
Spokes
Spigots
Stakes
Showcases
Screens
Stands
Stools
Swings
Sofas
Store fixtures
Shelving
Shakes
Shingles
Sash
Shutters
Slats for venetian blinds
Structural timbers
Sauna baths
Tanks
Toothpicks
Trays
Trophy bases
Tables
Tea wagons
Tubs
Unfinished furniture
Window frames
Woodblock flooring
Wardrobes
Whatnot shelves

4
WHERE TO LOCATE

Once you've decided what kind of business you want to start, the next most important decision is where to locate it. A poor choice can mean the difference between success and failure. Now, budget or personal considerations may restrict your choice in locating in the very best location. However, you should be aware of what you can do under the best of conditions, and compare that with the circumstances you are willing to settle for. After all, some new competitor may move into that ideal location and take away all your business? You don't want that to happen, but if it does, you want to know that you can still come up with a means of competing against that location effectively.

Let's look at the factors to consider when deciding on a location. This actually becomes two separate problems, depending on whether you intend to operate a retail or service establishment serving the local community, or to start some type of manufacturing operation, wholesale operation, or tourist recreation business. For those who are able, it may be advantageous to operate your business from your home. (We will deal with this in the next chapter.)

a. RETAIL AND SERVICE BUSINESSES
1. Trade area
In the last chapter, I presented the data published by the Small Business Administration on the number of inhabitants needed to support many different types of retail businesses. To make full use of that data, you need to know the population trends in the area you're considering. Such data is available on a county-by-county basis. Using this, you can analyze your county to see whether it can support one more of the particular type of business you propose to start.

POPULATION TRENDS IN OREGON
(According to County)

County	1970	1975
Baker	14,919	14,250
Benton	53,776	57,000
Clackamas	166,088	183,200
Clatsop	28,473	31,300
Columbia	28,790	31,650
Coos	56,515	58,100
Crook	9,985	10,500
Curry	13,006	13,500
Deschutes	30,442	33,100
Douglas	71,743	72,900
Gilliam	2,342	2,300
Grant	6,996	6,250
Harney	7,215	7,550
Hood River	13,187	13,300
Jackson	94,533	101,150
Jefferson	8,548	9,400
Josephine	35,746	38,000
Klamath	50,021	51,700
Lake	6,343	6,050
Lane	213,358	236,000
Lincoln	25,755	27,050
Linn	71,914	72,400
Malheur	23,169	23,150
Marion	151,309	165,000
Morrow	4,465	4,270
Multnomah	556,677	588,000
Polk	35,349	36,500
Sherman	2,139	2,100
Tillamook	17,930	17,990
Umatilla	44,923	45,500
Union	19,377	19,500
Wallowa	6,247	5,800
Wasco	20,133	20,600
Washington	157,920	175,000
Wheeler	1,849	1,840
Yamhill	40,213	44,100

2. Competition

Look at the quality and quantity of competition in the area where you want to locate. Are there any rumors of some big chain store coming in that would compete against you?

Do the businesses you'll be competing with stay open evenings or Sundays? Do they carry a wide selection of goods?

3. Community attitude

Do you detect any animosity toward your type of business in the area? If this is very pronounced, you had better look elsewhere. They'll probably never patronize your establishment. Maybe your competitor is a person who grew up in the area, and has such a strong attachment with the people in the neighborhood that they would never think of patronizing someone else.

4. Accessibility

Retail businesses must have customers coming in the door to survive. How do you accomplish this? Well, you have to do two things. First, you should locate where your type of customer would normally be passing by. Second, you should make it convenient for them to get to your store. Both automobile and pedestrian traffic patterns need to be studied. If they drive right past your door, is there a convenient place to park? How about bus stops? Are they close by?

5. General condition of the area

Are you locating in an area that will attract the type of customers that you need? Some businesses need to locate in prestige areas. Others, such as building material suppliers, can easily locate in less pretentious areas. However, you should look at the general area to decide whether it's going downhill in appearance, if vacancy rates are going up, and whether vandalism is rampant. Such areas obviously need new life in them. But don't expect your small beginning business to provide that spark. You have enough problems to deal with just getting started. Don't try to tackle the community's problems at the same time!

6. Proximity to competition

This is a knotty problem. Should you get as far away from all the competition as possible to capture a geographic advantage in a certain area? Or should you be as close as possible so that you can tap the stream of customers already going to their store, by inviting comparison shopping? A small all-night grocery can locate near a major supermarket (and still remain in business). That way, it is visible to all the supermarket's customers, who will remember it when they discover late at night that there is nothing in the house for breakfast.

7. Zoning

Is the current zoning in the area appropriate for your business? Can you expect other businesses to locate in the area to enhance your location?

8. Traffic analysis

Analysis of traffic is essential to determine just how many potential customers are actually passing your door. You should conduct two separate counts: one for pedestrians and one for automobiles. Both should be determined on an hourly basis. It will do little good if 1,000 cars pass each day, but 950 of them are part of a traffic flurry early in the morning and again in the evening.

When it comes to pedestrian count, you need to be selective. Having 1,000 people pass a women's dress shop each day wouldn't be much help if 900 of them were men! Again, the time is important. Early mornig passersby are obviously on their way to work. Noon-time passersby are on their way to lunch. They probably won't be your customers, unless you plan to open a lunch counter.

Finally, does the pedestrian traffic favor your side of the street? If all the nice stores are across the street, shoppers may never get over to your side.

9. Cost

Probably any retail business would attract the greatest number of customers if it were located in a major shopping center. That's where the crowds are, where all the factors I've discussed have been analyzed and taken care of by experts. It's also where the cost of space will undoubtedly be the highest. There's the rub. Will you really attract enough extra business to pay for all that extra rent? Will you be able to find the financing to go really first-class right off the bat? Only you can answer those questions.

b. MANUFACTURING AND WHOLESALE OPERATIONS

Locating manufacturing and wholesale operations is a challenging business that requires a great deal of investigation and analysis. Here, we'll discuss the factors relating primarily to manufacturing. However, many of these same rules apply to wholesale operations.

You might say that there are five M's that go into making any product: men (or women), materials, machines, management, and money. The output of all this effort will be "merchandise," which must have a "market" to provide the "motive" for the whole operation to work (three more M's). In other words, there must be enough profit to pay for the salaries of management, wages of workers, and dividends for those investing money in the business.

go into a manufacturing business. Today, it's considerably more complex than that. Oh, those eight M's are still a very important part of it. But today's manufacturers have a whole series of new concerns: the site itself, plant layout and design, equipment design or selection, transportation facilities and costs, environmental regulations, product regulations, unionization, taxes, suppliers, support facilities, utilities, and sources of energy.

The wise manufacturer will attempt to find the location which will minimize the costs and the problems involved in *all* these various factors.

1. Site factors

Assuming that you're going to have to build something fairly special for your plant, ask these questions concerning the following:

(a) **The soil:**
   (i) What is the maximum loading?
   (ii) Will you need any fill?
   (iii) Will any compaction be required?
   (iv) Are there any rock outcroppings at awkward locations?
   (v) Will piling be required to support any structures?
   (vi) If you need septic tanks, what is the permeability?

(b) **The configuration:**
   (i) What are the dimensions?
   (ii) How about the slope?
   (iii) Are there any drainage problems?
   (iv) Will substantial grading be required?
   (v) Are there any existing buildings?
   (vi) Can they be used, or do they have to be torn down?
   (vii) Is there any timber to be removed?

(c) **The surroundings:**
   (i) Is there room for future expansion?
   (ii) Are the neighbors compatible?
   (iii) Is the area subject to flooding?
   (iv) Do you have proximity to a major supplier or customer?

(d) **The zoning:**
   (i) Is it suitable for your type of operation?
   (ii) Will it restrict you from a future course of expansion?

(e) **The cost:**
   (i) In addition to the basic purchase cost, is there a large preparation cost?
   (ii) Are construction costs going to be unusually high or low?
   (iii) Are any special financing or leasing arrangements available?

2. **Transportation**

   (a) **Railroads:**
   - (i) Is rail on or available to the site?
   - (ii) What are the freight rates for your product to your markets?
   - (iii) What sort of switching service is available?
   - (iv) Who installs spur track?
   - (v) Who maintains spurs?
   - (vi) Will you have service by more than one railroad?

   (b) **Motor freight:**
   - (i) What are the freight rates for your product to your market?
   - (ii) Do you have convenient access to a freeway?
   - (iii) What are the delivery schedules?
   - (iv) Is there more than one local carrier that can carry your product?
   - (v) What delivery zone are you in with regard to your major suppliers?

   (c) **Water transportation:**
   - (i) Are you close to an established marine terminal?
   - (ii) Do you need your own dock?
   - (iii) What is the minimum draft that you need?
   - (iv) What are the tidal variations?
   - (v) What are your shipping costs going to be?
   - (vi) Are there any port charges?

   (d) **Air transportation:**
   - (i) How far is it to the nearest major airport?
   - (ii) How much are air freight costs for your products?
   - (iii) Are there convenient schedules to the other places you need to fly to?

3. **Environmental considerations**
   (a) **Physical:**
   - (i) What are the present pollutants in the air and water in the area?
   - (ii) If you're going to be discharging any yourself, will it exceed the maximum allowable concentrations set by the Department of Ecology or the local air pollution control authority?
   - (iii) Will your discharge of warm water exceed thermal standards?
   - (iv) Will you have any odors or noise that would be objectionable to neighbors?

   (b) **Climate:**
   - (i) What are the temperature extremes in the area? Will these affect your product or productivity of workers?
   - (ii) How about wind, rainfall, and snowfall? Will these require special construction?

   (c) **Social:**
   Will the community welcome your plant?

   (d) **Political**
   - (i) Does state and local legislation indicate an anti-industry attitude?
   - (ii) Is there pro-labor legislation which might affect your operations?

4. **Regulations**

In chapter 6 we'll discuss in more detail the regulations you will need to be concerned with here in Oregon. You should keep all these in mind as you look for a suitable location. By locating in certain areas, you will eliminate or at least minimize the impact of some of these regulations.

5. **Taxes**

In chapter 10 we'll be discussing taxes in some detail. I would call to your attention the comparison of local property tax rates for the various counties in that chapter. You will note quite a variation which may be important to your type of business.

6. **Labor**
   (a) What is the availability of the types of workers you need?
   (b) What are the prevailing wage rates in the area?
   (c) How productive are the workers in the area?
   (d) What is their educational level?
   (e) Is there a high degree of unionization in the area?
   (f) Which unions are most active in the area?
   (g) Will workers move to your area from outside?

7. **Utilities**
   (a) **Drinking water supply:**
       (i) What size main is available?
       (ii) How much pressure does it have?
       (iii) What is its maximum flow?
       (iv) If you have boilers, you'll need to know the chemical analysis.
       (v) What is the price?
   (b) **Water for fire protection:**
       (i) What size main is available?
       (ii) How much pressure does it have?
       (iii) How large a reservoir backs it up?
       (iv) Can water be fed in from two directions?
   (c) **Sewage disposal:**
       (i) What size sewer main is available?
       (ii) How deep is it?
       (iii) What type of treatment plant does it tie into?
       (iv) Are there any limitations on what you can discharge into it?
       (v) How are charges determined?
       (vi) Are septic tanks allowed in the area?

(d) Telephone service:
  (i) How far does local service cover?
  (ii) Will the local telephone company provided the special in-plant features you are interested in?

8. Energy

The days of plentiful power are gone, until we are able to come up with acceptable sources of new energy. With our supply of hydro-electric power here in the Pacific Northwest, we are a little better off than other parts of the country. Our power companies can still supply reasonable increments on demand. Some can do more than others, so you need to check availability. Sometimes, this is on a firm basis; other times, on an interruptible basis. Check the basis for charges. Ask for a report on the future outlook for continued service at the level you require in that area.

The supply of natural gas is completely dependent on external sources for continued service. Except for very minimal quantities for heating purposes, don't count on anything more than interruptible supplies. Check into the expected number of days of interruption. This will vary with different utility companies, who have different means for taking care of peak demands.

Don't automatically assume that fuel oil or LPG are readily available as substitutes for natural gas. Check with local dealers. Are they willing to take you on as a customer with the same ration privileges as all their current customers, in case another boycott occurs? Remember, we're more dependent on Arab oil now than ever before.

However, we do have fair supplies of coal here in the Northwest. Consider designing your plant to use this resource. If you do, then check out the best sources for this material.

9. Suppliers

Before locating anywhere, be sure to check into your supplier situation. This includes not only your raw materials, but your operating supplies and your maintenance supplies. Check on local suppliers for such things as: pipes and fittings, electrical supplies, bearings, V-belts, mechanical transmission equipment, material handling equipment, lubricants, boiler supplies, general hardware, and building supplies.

10. Support services

Sometimes, the prices on industrial land in larger cities look unbelievably high. This makes locations in smaller cities look very good. But it does bring up the value of the many support services you will need to call on from time to time. If they're not nearby, you will be paying a premium cost every time you do need them. Consider how often you may need to use the services of: machine shops, welding shops, mechanical contractors, security services, fire departments, hospitals, crane services, computer services, special skills, and service representatives.

c. TOURIST RECREATION BUSINESSES

There's no denying that Oregon is a tourists' paradise. Every year, thousands of travelers make the trek across mountains, prairies, and deserts just to enjoy a few days in this scenic state. Spending in Oregon by out-of-state visitors is another rapidly growing goldmine. Take a look at them!

VALUE OF OUT-OF-STATE VISITORS TO OREGON

1963	$219,700,000
1964	244,700,000
1965	250,459,000
1966	252,700,000
1967	258,569,000
1968	285,622,000
1969	326,435,000
1970	339,465,000
1971	438,261,000

Source: Oregon State Highway Division, Planning Section — Economics Unit, *1971 Out-of-state Tourist Revenue Study*, (Salem, OR: Oregon State Highway Division, 1971), p. 3.

Where can you locate to tap into this goldmine? Well, the answer is fairly obvious. You locate where the tourists are already going. But do you know where they are? Oh, sure we know they come to see the ocean beaches and Mount Hood and Crater Lake. Where else? It wouldn't work out very well if all the tourist businesses were located in just those locations. Many would go broke there while the tourists would be poorly served in other locations. You don't necessarily have to be at the main attractions to serve the traveling public. They need to eat, sleep, buy gas, and so on all along the way.

The trick then is to know where the main travel routes are. In 1971 the Oregon State Highway Division made a detailed survey of this by interviewing parties leaving the state at every exit location (on a sampling basis). The results give some pretty good clues as to where the tourists are travelling.

This same study came up with some other interesting statistics. The type of lodging used included: motels — 30%, friends — 23.2%, hotels — 1.3%, camping — 24.1%, house trailers — 2.8%, second house in Oregon — 0.6%, no housing — 18.0%.

Those using Oregon campgrounds utilized private campgrounds 20.4% of the time. Expenditures for food and automobile expenses were about 70% of the total money spent by tourists.

NUMBER OF TRAVELERS BY LOCATION AND ROUTE, AND AVERAGE DAYS SPENT AND MILES TRAVELED IN OREGON

Location	Route	Estimated Number of Persons	Average Miles in Oregon	Average Days in Oregon
Brookings	US 101, S. Exit	616,805	467	4.6
O'Brien	US 199	333,443	363	3.4
Ashland	I-5, S. Exit	1,593,145	416	4.3
Worden	US 97, S. Exit	270,888	406	4.1
Merrill	ORE 39	238,124	485	5.5
Cairo Junction	US 20	183,296	470	4.4
Olds Ferry	I-80N	499,152	360	3.6
Milton-Freewater	ORE 11	203,427	406	3.3
Cold Springs	US 730	376,345	419	3.0
Sam Hill Mem. Bridge	US 97, N. Exit	161,241	383	2.3
The Dalles Bridge	US 197	119,360	433	3.0
Hood River Bridge		145,606	374	2.5
Bridge of Gods		49,682	364	4.6
Interstate Bridge	I-5, N. Exit	2,848,318	396	2.8
Longview Bridge		288,248	467	5.7
Astoria Bridge	US 101, N. Exit	199,880	423	3.1
Umatilla		398,143	375	2.8
Other Routes		567,679	415	3.9
TOTAL		9,092,782	409	3.4

Source: Oregon State Highway Division, Planning Section — Economics Unit, *1971 Out-of-state Tourist Revenue Study,* (Salem, OR: Oregon State Highway Division, 1971), p. 16.

5
OPERATING A BUSINESS FROM YOUR HOME

In chapter 4 we discussed the important considerations in locating your business. Some of you may not have much choice. For example, if you want to get into the auto-wrecking business, there are very definite zoning restrictions on where you can operate. The same is true for any heavy industry, or business which involves a physical plant of any size, or which may cause a nuisance in a residential neighborhood. As we saw in chapter 5, for some people, location is one of the most important decisions. However, for others, it is not, and those people should consider (where it is practicable) locating in the home.

Operating a business from your home is not very different from operating a business from an office, warehouse, or shop anywhere else. But the advantages to be gained from doing business at home are almost too numerous to mention. The main advantages are these:

(a) You do away with traffic problems.
(b) You save money because you travel less.
(c) You can claim a portion of your home expenses as a tax deduction.
(d) You save time.

You can operate almost any kind of business from home. The majority of home-based businesses, however, fall under one of the following headings:

(a) Services
(b) Personal skills (professionally applied)
(c) Mail order
(d) Light manufacturing

Hence, one of the first and most vital decisions you have to make is whether to operate out of your home or whether to rent outside space. Again, sometimes you will have no choice if, for example, you are starting a retail business or manufacturing concern which simply cannot be fitted into the basement. Or, perhaps you live in a small, one-bedroom apartment, and it is simply impossible to expropriate space for your business. If you employ outside help, it will be more difficult to operate out of the house unless, of course, you employ only salespeople who are on the road all the time.

Consider, also, that you will need a business license, and that each city has regulations regarding the type of business you may operate out of a home. These regulations are not normally enforced too strenuously unless you become a nuisance to a neighbor, in which case the city has to act. So be careful.

Besides these considerations, the choice should be based on your personal needs and requirements. You may feel that you need office space for prestige reasons. Or you may feel that you simply do not have the self-discipline to avoid the many distractions that exist at home.

However, you should know by now that one of the main reasons for even starting your own business should be to cut expenses, avoid heavy traffic, and make more money. Moreover, the time you spend driving from home to office or factory is wasted time!

For argument's sake, let's break down the factors involved in this decision. (The same method can be used even if comparing two *rented* premises.)

a. RENTED PREMISES

You have to pay rent, spend money on reasonable office furnishings, travel to and from your place of business, and pay utility bills. Let's break this down even further. Time is money. The time you spend travelling to and from your rented office is lost time. Also, travelling expenses will eat into your profits.

What if your new business doesn't pan out as expected? The money you laid out for rent, telephone, heat and light, office furniture, and travelling is lost money. However, if your business grows and makes money, you still have those fixed expenses. They cannot decrease. Most likely, your expenses will increase, eating ever deeper into your profits. You will have to earn more money in order to meet these fixed expenses. Any money that you pay out for the fixed expenses described above is money lost — money that you earned but cannot use.

b. OPERATING AT HOME

By working at home, you actually cut your usual home expenses because you can claim a portion as a tax deduction when you use a room at home for business purposes. (See section b. of chapter 12 for a fuller discussion of the tax advantages.)

Here's some proof to show you that you save money and make more money, working your business in your home. Let's list the expenses involved in operating from a rented office downtown.

Office rent	$210 per month
Telephone	$ 50 per month
Utilities	$ 20 per month
Travelling	$ 50 per month
Lunches	$ 50 per month

You could possibly save $420 monthly by operating at home — maybe more, if you evaluate your time lost travelling. So, if your aim is to make $300 per week running your own business, then isn't it more profitable to operate at home? Haven't you already made $420 because you saved the above-mentioned expenses? Of course you have.

In operating any type of business, a prime objective should be to cut expenses and increase profits. The main reason for even being in business is to make as much money with the least outlay in as short a time as possible. If, by operating from your home, you can cut expenses without decreasing efficiency, then this is what you should do at least until business growth demands otherwise.

By operating at home, you can:
(a) Begin part-time
(b) Operate with small overhead
(c) Control expansion completely
(d) Do everything yourself
(e) Start with very little capital
(f) Accomplish more in less time

The fact that you operate from your home can add two hours per day to working time. Suppose you work for someone else from nine to five? That's eight hours. Add travelling time and expenses, and you will see what I mean. You will use up at least ten hours of every day with two hours' unpaid time wasted! If you waste two hours each day travelling to and from your place of business, this adds up to 520 hours down the drain in one year!

The average person works about 45 years in a lifetime. By losing 520 hours annually in traveling time, you actually waste about 23,400 hours in your lifetime. Just by working at home you can add those wasted hours to your business or use those hours in leisure time with your family!

Here is something startling. Very few home businesses fail. Why is this? By operating at home you cut expenses and you do everything yourself. You know and control every phase of your business, and you waste very little money on employees who are interested only in their own welfare!

Yet, how many people do you know who operate a business from their home? The kinds of businesses run from one room in a private home are in the thousands. Here are just a few "home operators" that I know of personally:
(a) Plumbers
(b) Carpenters
(c) Insurance agents
(d) Real estate agents
(e) Doctors

(f) Dentists
(g) Boat builders
(h) Mechanics (automotive, electrical, marine)
(i) Typists
(j) Farmers
(k) Private detectives
(l) Beauty parlors

They are happier, more successful, have more free time to spend with their families, and live longer than any other self-employed group I know! If you took the time to do a little research, you would make a rather startling discovery. Almost any kind of service or "skills" business can be operated successfully from your home.

The prime example is the mail-order business person who makes a good living selling products, books, services, and information by mail — operating in a room in the basement, attic, or even from a kitchen table.

The service business in America is growing faster than the population. Americans spend millions upon millions of dollars annually for services that are taken for granted. Often, money spent on such services as dry-cleaning, laundering, car repairs, house repairs, medical services, and information and writing services is greater than the amount of money spent on food.

One fellow I know is a repairman, making a killing repairing all sorts of small appliances. He works from his basement! And you can do the same. Do what you do best for a reasonable fee. Keep expenses down and you've got it made. That is the case for "operating-at-home" versus doing business from high rental premises downtown. Think it over carefully. Then pick the "place of business" that is *best* for you.

c. WHEN NOT TO USE YOUR HOME

Before we leave this chapter, we should also consider the reasons for not using your home for business. There does have to be a balance between business and personal goals.

You do want to be successful in business, but at the same time you should want a successful family life. The two goals shouldn't have to be in conflict. Let's face it: togetherness is great up to a point. Beyond that, it can become a real source of irritation. Both you and your spouse may need more time to yourselves than working at home would allow.

You probably already know whether this would be a problem in your marriage. Do you tend to get on each other's nerves by the end of a weekend? Do you tend to look for reasons to get out of the house alone? If so, you should think twice about working at home.

How well-behaved are your children? Do they understand that things on your desk or workbench are not to be disturbed? How noisy are they around the house? Can you work under those conditions effectively? Can you concentrate on work when there's just the normal talking, singing, fussing, crying, etc.? If you are easily distracted, don't let these kinds of problems jeopardize the success of your business.

6
HOW TO GET STARTED

a. FOLLOWING THE RULES AND REGULATIONS

Establishing a business in any state involves contacting a number of different federal, state, and local agencies to see that all pertinent rules and regulations are being followed. In this chapter, I'll outline all those rules and regulations currently applicable in the state of Oregon. Appropriate agencies to contact are shown along with current fees.

Some contacts are routine, involving nothing more than providing relevant information and paying the necessary fees. Others are more complex, and may involve several contacts and substantial work before the necessary permits are granted. Anyone proposing to start a new business should plan to contact these agencies as early as possible to make certain that the time involved in obtaining these permits does not delay the overall project unduly. These agencies include: the Environmental Protection Agency; the Corps of Engineers; the Department of Environmental Quality; the Corporation Commissioner for sale of securities; local planning departments; and local building departments.

b. WHAT KIND OF BUSINESS ORGANIZATION?

1. Sole proprietorships

Sole proprietorships are the most common and simplest form of business organization. You may start such a business with little or no formalities, preferably after consulting your lawyer and accountant. Business licenses are required by most municipalities. If you have any employees, you will need to register your Employer's Registration Report for Oregon Withholding Tax and/or Tri-County Metropolitan Transportation District of Oregon Excise Tax with the Department of Revenue.

If you intend to operate under an assumed name, you will also need to register that name with the Corporation Commissioner. Otherwise you will only need those specialized licenses that may be required for the particular activities you wish to engage in.

2. Partnerships

A partnership is an association of two or more persons to transact business. Partnerships in Oregon are regulated by the "Uniform Partnership Law," which has been adopted by many other states. Partnership agreements should be in a written form to define clearly the rights and responsibilities of each partner. However, in lieu of formal agreements provisions of the Uniform Partnership Act will apply and do not need to be included in the agreement.

(a) What kind: general or limited?

There are two basic types which can be set up: either a general partnership or a limited partnership, whichever is selected by personal agreement between the partners. (Consultation with an attorney is recommended.) In a general partnership the partners are each liable for the obligations incurred by the firm. If the firm is unable to meet its obligations, creditors may take action against each partner personally.

No permission is required from the state to form a general partnership. However, if the partnership takes an assumed name, that must be registered with the Corporation Commissioner.

If the business is a limited partnership, then each partner shares an agreed percentage of profits and assumes an agreed percentage of personal liability. These do not necessarily have to be the same percentages. At least one general partner must be subject to all liabilities. Normally a limited partner is one who invests in the business but does not wish to assume liabilities beyond the amount of investment.

Limited partnerships must be registered with the Corporation Commissioner, Department of Commerce, Corporation Division, Commerce Building, 158 — 12th St. N.E., Salem, Oregon 97310. The filing fee is $25.00.

(b) Registering an assumed name

Chances are your parents spent months deciding what your name should be. You've lived with their decision all your life and you're probably very comfortable with it. However, when it comes to starting a business you need to give some serious thought to whether that name will be the best one for your business — particularly if you have a name that is long or difficult to spell. Then you should give some thought to using something else. A catchy name that ties in well with your type of business can be a definite asset.

As I mentioned earlier, if you are starting a sole proprietorship or a partnership under an assumed name, you will need to register it with the Corporation Commissioner. These assumed names are indexed along with corporation names, limited partnerships, and trade service marks to protect them from encroachment or mistaken identity.

What constitutes an assumed name? Your real name, standing alone, and coupled only with words which describe the business would not be considered an assumed name. By "real name," the law means your surname coupled with one or more given names or initials, or any combination thereof. For example, "Bill" J. Jones, Radio

Repair would not be considered an assumed name. However, "Jones Radio Repair" would be.

Any time you use the words "Company", "& Company", "& Sons", "& Associates" or the like you will need to register. Fees are $5.00 plus $1.50 for each county you intend to operate in. They cover a five-year period.

3. Corporations

The third major form of business organization is the corporation. In this type of organization the corporation itself becomes a legal entity, removing the stockholder from any personal liability for debts incurred. Generally speaking the stockholder only stands to lose whatever investment was made in the corporation. A corporation provides the ability to raise capital through the sale of stock. However, there is a price to pay for this freedom from liability. It comes in the form of additional regulations, taxes directly on the corporation, and annual license fees. (More of this later.)

c. FORMING A CORPORATION

Any group deciding to establish a corporation may do so by filing their articles of incorporation with:

The Corporation Commissioner
Department of Commerce, Corporation Division
Commerce Building
158 — 12th St. N.E.
Salem, Oregon 97310

Required forms are available from that office.

One or more persons aged 18 or over may incorporate a business by filling out this form in duplicate. Information to be supplied includes the following:

(1) The name of the corporation.
This must be different and not deceptively similar to the name of any other corporation, limited partnership, reserved or registered name on file with the Corporation Commissioner. A name may be reserved for a 120-day

period ahead of actual incorporation by filing an application with the Corporation Commissioner and paying a $5.00 fee.

(2) The planned duration of the corporation.
This will normally be stated as perpetual.

(3) The purpose or purposes for which the corporation is organized.
It is enough to state, either alone or with other purposes: "That the corporation may engage in any lawful activity for which corporations may be organized under ORS Chapter 57." However, it is desirable to state the primary purpose along with this statement.

(4) The aggregate number of shares which the corporation shall have authority to issue.
Here you will have to indicate whether the shares are to have a par value or not, what that par value is, and if there is to be more than one class of shares. If there is more than one class, then the preference, limitations, and relative rights of each class must be stated.

(5) The address of the initial registered office.
(6) The name of the initial registered agent.
(7) The numer of directors constituting the initial board of directors.
(8) The names and addresses of initial directors.
(9) The name and address of each incorporator.
(10) Provisions for regulating internal affairs of the corporation as may be appropriate.

If the Corporation Commissioner determines that the articles conform to law, a certificate of incorporation will be issued after payment of the required fees. These include the filing fee and the first annual license fee. Both are based on the value of authorized shares as follows:

Value of shares	Filing Fee	License Fee	Total Fee
$5,000 or under	$ 10	$ 10	$ 20
$5,000 to $10,000	$ 15	$ 15	$ 30
$10,000 to $25,000	$ 20	$ 20	$ 40
$25,000 to $50,000	$ 30	$ 30	$ 60
$50,000 to $100,000	$ 50	$ 50	$100
$100,000 to $250,000	$ 75	$ 75	$150
$250,000 to $500,000	$100	$100	$200
$500,000 to $1,000,000	$125	$125	$250
Over $1,000,000	$200	$200	$400

To determine the amount owed by a corporation having stock with no par value, an arbitrary $10 value is assigned to each share.

The corporation comes into existence when the certificate of incorporation is issued. However, the corporation may not transact business or incur debts until at least $1,000 has been paid for shares. If the total value of authorized shares is less than $1,000, then the total par value of the shares must be paid in. Once this minimum amount of capital is accumulated, you are ready to take the next step in organizing. This involves calling the first meeting of the board of directors to elect officers and adopt by-laws. Every corporation must have at least a president and secretary, and these must be two different persons. Other officers are optional and one person may hold more than one office if desired. Having done all this you are now ready to transact business in the state of Oregon. Whenever you expand or find it necessary, for one reason or another, to operate in other states, you will need to go through a similar process to transact business there.

d. THE SALE OF SECURITIES

The rules and regulations pertaining to the sale of securities involve a highly specialized branch of law practice. It is beyond the scope of this book to do much more than indicate the agencies involved.

When sales are strictly limited to residents of the state of Oregon, you will only need to register with:

The Corporation Commissioner
Department of Commerce, Corporation Division
Commerce Building
158 — 12th Street, N.E.
Salem, Oregon 97310

For interstate sales it will also be necessary to register with the federal offices of the Securities and Exchange Commission. That agency maintains an office in Seattle, Washington.

Anyone needing detailed information on state laws on this subject should refer to chapter 59 of the Oregon Revised Statutes. Be aware that there are severe penalties for violations of the Securities Law.

e. AUTHORIZATION FOR OUT-OF-STATE CORPORATIONS TO TRANSACT BUSINESS IN OREGON

Any foreign corporation wishing to conduct business in Oregon must obtain a certificate of authority from the Corporation Commissioner. The filing fee for this certificate is $40. The annual license fee is $200 regardless of the amount of authorized stock which must also be paid initially. Each foreign corporation so authorized must maintain a registered office and registered agent in Oregon.

Once this certificate is issued, the foreign corporation enjoys the same rights and privileges as an Oregon corporation. Like the domestic corporation, the foreign corporation must file an annual report.

Certain activities are not considered business transactions under Oregon law and do not require certificates of authority. These include: court actions; meetings of directors; maintaining a bank account; maintaining offices for transfer, exchange, and registration of corporate securities; sales through independent contractors; soliciting or procuring orders which require acceptance outside of Oregon before becoming binding contracts; borrowing money; interstate commerce; and isolated transactions completed within 30 days.

f. STATE AND FEDERAL REQUIREMENTS

1. Department of Revenue

Every employer in Oregon must apply for an account number for the Oregon Withholding Tax and/or Tri-County Metropolitan Transportation District of Oregon Excise Tax. This is done by filing Form W55 with the Department of Revenue, P.O. Box 800, Salem, Oregon 97308. Copies of this form are obtained by writing to this office or by contacting district offices in Astoria, Bend, Coos Bay, Corvallis, Eugene, Hillsboro, Klamath Falls, Medford, Ontario, Oregon City, Pendleton, Portland, Roseburg, The Dalles, or Salem.

Employers must withhold tax from each employee's wages at the time of payment. The amount may be determined on a percentage basis or by wage bracket tables. (**Caution:** The employer becomes liable for any taxes not withheld. These withholdings must be set aside and held in trust until the due date for remittance.) Monthly, quarterly, and annual reports and remittances are required depending on amounts withheld.)

2. Workers' compensation insurance

Every business employing one or more persons in Oregon is required to carry workers' compensation insurance — with certain exceptions. This can be done in one of three ways:

(a) By purchasing insurance from any private insurer approved by the Oregon Insurance Commissioner.

(b) By becoming a self-insurer. This involves providing cash, security deposit, or surety bond requirements (minimum $100,000) to be held by the Workers-Compensation Board to guarantee payments for injuries and diseases of occupational origin incurred by employees.

(c) By purchasing coverage under the State Accident Insurance Fund. This is a state agency which operates as a mutual insurance company. Application may be made at offices located in Astoria, Bend, Baker, Beaverton, Corvallis, Eugene, Klamath Falls, Medford, Milwaukie, North Bend, Pendleton, Portland, Roseburg, Salem, and The Dalles. Rates vary according to the type of industry involved and will improve with favorable experience. Premium discounts are allowed for premiums over $1,000. Underwriting profit and investment income are returned to policyholders as dividends.

3. Department of Human Resources, Employment Division requirements and assistance

(a) Unemployment insurance

Every employer of one or more persons employed at least 20 weeks during a calendar year must register for unemployment insurance. Firms with a payroll of $225 in any calendar quarter are also subject to this insurance requirement.

The cost for this insurance is paid solely by the employer. The normal contribution is 2.7% of the first $8,000 paid to each employee during each calendar year. This varies, however, depending on experience. Employers with good experience ratings may receive reductions of up to 2.6% of the first $8,000.

Employers with poor experience ratings will be subject to increases in contributions of up to 4% of the first $8,000 paid to each employee.

This experience rating is based on the number of claims paid to your former employees over a three-year period. This is something to keep in mind when you think about hiring and laying off employees. You could be paying a penalty for quite a few years for making poor decisions here.

Application for an unemployment insurance account is made by filing a copy of the Status Report, Form 12 with the Employment Division. Offices are located in Albany, Astoria, Baker, Bend, Coos Bay, Corvallis, Eugene, Grants Pass, Gresham, Hermiston, Hillsboro, Hood River, Klamath Falls La Grande, Lakeview, Lebanon, McMinnville, Medford, Milton-Freewater, Ontario, Oregon City, Pendleton, Portland, Roseburg, St. Helens, Salem, The Dalles, Tillamook, and Toledo.

(b) Assistance

Worker Recruitment — Local Employment Division offices maintain files on individuals seeking jobs. These job candidates are pre-screened for any job listed by an employer. If qualified workers are not available locally, recruitment can be extended to other locations. In case of shortages of qualified applicants, aptitude tests will be given to select suitable candidates for training programs.

New employers should be aware of the following training programs available through the Employment Division.

1. Work Incentive Program (WIN-OJT) — This is for both individuals receiving aid and families with dependent children. The employer who provides on-the-job training for Work Incentive Program participants is entitled to reimbursement for training costs for an amount equal to 50% of the employee's starting wage. In addition, employers may be reimbursed for 100% of the wages for the time the participant is released from work to attend an approved job-related education class of up to 10 hours per week for 26 weeks. The cost for job-related education may be paid from Work Incentive Program funds under separate contract.

In addition, the Revenue Act of 1971 offers substantial tax credits to employers of persons given on-the-job training under the Work Incentive Program. Generally, the act permits an employer of an individual who has participated in the Work Incentive Program to claim a total tax credit of 20% of the individual's first 12 months' salary or wages, provided that the employment continues for another 12 months.

The employer does not have to repay the tax credits if the employee leaves voluntarily, becomes disabled during the period, or is fired for misconduct, as determined under the state's unemployment compensation laws.

2. Jobs Optional Program (JOP) — This program offers employers the opportunity to hire and train a specified number of unskilled persons for permanent employment in jobs that provide an opportunity for advancement. The program also enables employers to upgrade present employees into occupations requiring higher skills or into jobs where there is a shortage of skilled workers.

3. National Alliance of Businessmen (NAB) — This program represents a combined nation-wide effort of the federal government and private industry to make job opportunities in the business sector a reality for the nation's disadvantaged workers.

It is available to employers who desire to hire, train, or upgrade and provide supportive services to the disadvantaged. The cost of training, remedial education, correction of minor health problems, personnel counselling and testing, transportation, day care, and other services may be covered.

The employer may be reimbursed for 1/2 the beginning wage, which must be $2.00 per hour or more, and the cost of all other supportive services given. The training program should be no less than eight weeks or more than 45 weeks, with the length of the training period dependent upon the complexity of the occupation.

4. Department of Agriculture

The State Department of Agriculture is the prime contact for all food-related businesses and occupations. Licenses and permits are required from this department for the following businesses:

Abattoirs
Apiaries
Auction yards

Bakeries
Carbonated beverage plants
Cat and dog food canneries
Commercial feed
Commercial fertilizer
Custom slaughterers
Dairy products
Economic poisons
Egg dealers
Food establishments
Grade A fluid milk
Food processors
Frozen dairy desserts
Garbage feeders
Meat dealers
Non-slaughtering processing plants
Nurseries
Poultry or rabbit slaughterers
Produce
Public warehouses
Refrigerated lockers
Rendering plants
Seed dealers
Slaughterhouses
Weights and measures

In addition, the department examines individuals and issues licenses to qualified applicants who wish to work in the following occupations:

Buttermakers
Cheesemakers
Cream graders
Livestock weighers
Milk graders
Milk samplers
Pasteurizer operators
Pesticide applicators
Pesticide operators

The main office for the department is:
Department of Agriculture
Agriculture Building
Salem, Oregon 97310
In Portland the address is:
726 S.E. 20th Street.

5. Department of Environmental Quality

Oregon's stated policy is to conserve all inland, coastal, and ground waters in the state and to maintain or improve their quality for all legitimate and beneficial uses. Reasonably pure air is also to be maintained to prevent possible injury to human, plant, or animal life. Economic and industrial well-being are, at least in theory, to be considered in these policies.

The regulation and control of air and water pollution is handled by the Department of Environmental Quality (DEQ) and regional authorities, which may be formed by municipalities in a given region. You must obtain a permit before doing any of the following:

(a) Discharging any sewage or wastes into state waters from any commercial or industrial facility

(b) Increasing the volume or strength of any waste above amounts specified on an existing permit

(c) Constructing, installing, or operating any industrial or commercial facility which will cause an increase in waste discharge into state waters above amounts previously authorized

(d) Constructing or using any new outlet for discharging wastes into state waters

(e) Locating, constructing, and operating solid waste disposal sites

(f) Constructing or using a subsurface sewage disposal system (Note: Some counties issue these permits under contract to DEQ.)

(h) Constructing any facility which will become a source of air contamination

(i) Burning open fields

(j) Conducting activities in wilderness areas

(k) Creating noise above certain levels

Since substantial costs are frequently encountered in purchasing and installing pollution control equipment, two forms of tax relief have been enacted in Oregon. First, a tax credit of up to 5% of the cost, but not exceeding the taxpayer's liability, may be deducted from either the corporate excise tax or personal income tax each year until 50% of the cost has been credited. The credit is in lieu of any depreciation deduction. Installation must be complete by December 31, 1980.

The second alternative is to take an *ad valorem* tax exemption (property tax) on the value of the pollution control equipment for a period of up to 20 years. Once made, the election of method of tax relief is irrevocable. Facilities and allowable credits must be certified by DEQ. (**Caution:** Pre-notification of intent to apply for a tax credit must be made before installation or construction. Failure to do so may result in loss of the credit.)

The Department of Environmental Quality is located at 2595 State Street, Salem, Oregon. District offices are located in Bend, Eugene, Pendleton, Portland, and Roseburg.

6. United States Army Corps of Engineers

A permit is required for any construction proposed on or in the navigable waters of any state. The Corps of Engineers has jurisdiction over the review of all such projects and issuance of permits. If any work is planned for the navigable waters of the Columbia River or tributaries west of John Day River or along the Pacific coast, it is advisable to contact:

Department of the Army
Corps of Engineers
Portland District
2850 S.E. 82nd Avenue
Portland, Oregon 97208

For projects planned in navigable waters of the Columbia River or tributaries east of and including the John Day River contact:

> Department of the Army
> Corps of Engineers
> Walla Walla District
> Building 602
> City-County Airport
> Walla Walla, Washington

Projects in the Klamath Falls area come under the jurisdiction of the San Francisco District:

> Department of the Army
> Corps of Engineers
> San Francisco District
> 100 McAlster
> San Francisco, California

The Oregon Department of Environmental Quality issues discharge permits under authority granted them by EPA. Veto power over any permit is retained by EPA. The Corps of Engineers will only become involved when the proposed discharge poses a hindrance to navigation.

The Corps of Engineers is also responsible for issuing waste discharge permits under an 1899 law. However, this responsibility has been transferred to the United States Environmental Protection Agency.

7. United States Environmental Protection Agency

The United States Environmental Protection Agency operates under the authority of the United States Environmental Policy Act. The state of Oregon has implemented a similar verison of the same legislation, under which authority for the enforcement of air and water standards rests with state and local authorities. The United States Army Corps of Engineers has transferred its responsibility for the review of applications for permits to discharge wastes into navigable bodies of waters to the Environmental Protection Agency.

The Environmental Protection Agency maintains an office at:
1234 S.W. Morrison
Portland, Oregon 97205

8. Occupational Safety and Health Administration (OSHA)

Probably no other program has created as much controversy as the Occupational Safety and Health Act. The act has imposed a very complex and demanding set of regulations on the nation's businesses. No licensing or registration is required initially. However, virtually any business having employees is subject to inspection at any time. Any violations of safety or health standards are cause for on-the-spot penalties. These can easily amount to hundreds and even thousands of dollars depending on the circumstances. Needless to say, it is imperative for a new employer to become acquainted with these standards ahead of time!

These standards and other responsibilities of employers are covered in the following booklets: "Record Keeping Requirements Under the Williams-Steiger Occupational Safety and Health Act of 1970," "Setting New Standards for Job Safety and Health," "Guidelines for Setting up Job Safety and Health Programs," and "Federal Register for Occupational Safety and Health Standards." All of these may be obtained from:
U.S. Department of Labor
Occupational Safety and Health Administration
Room 526, Pittock Block
921 S.W. Washington Street
Portland, Oregon 97205

In Oregon administration of the OSHA program is under control of the Accident Prevention Division, Oregon State Workmen's Compensation Board. For information on the program, contact that agency at Labor and Industries Building, Salem, Oregon 97310.

9. Other state licenses

In addition to those already mentioned, there are numerous other permits, registrations, certificates, and licenses required for various types of businesses and occupations. I have listed below the agency or board responsible for the licensing or registration and the occupations or activities controlled by that agency or board.

Oregon State Board of Accountancy
158 12th Street, N.E.
Salem, OR 97310
- Certified public accountant
- CPA partnership
- Declaration of Intent
- Municipal auditor
- Public accountant
- Public accountant partnership
- Professional corporation

Oregon State Board of Aeronautics
3040 25th Street S.E.
Salem, OR 97310
- Aeronautical schools
- Aircraft
- Airmen
- Airports/heliports
- Airport/heliport site approval
- Dealers
- Forest spray pilots

Oregon State Board of Architect Examiners
202 Commerce Building
Salem, OR 97310
- Architects

Oregon State Board of Aucitoneers
158 12th Street, N.E.
Salem, OR 97310
- Auctioneer
- Auctioneer trainee
- Auction mart operator

Oregon State Bar
808 S.W. 15th Avenue
Portland, OR 97205
- Attorney

Oregon State Board of Barber Examiners
State Office Building
1400 S.W. 5th Avenue
Portland, OR 97201
  Barber
  Barber apprentice
  Barber school or college
  Barber shop
  Barber teacher

Oregon State Board of Chiropractic Examiners
4445 Verda Lane, N.E.
Salem, OR 97303
  Chiropractor

Oregon State Board of Pilot Commissioners
Department of Commerce
State Office Building
1400 S.W. 5th Avenue
Portland, OR 97201
  River and bar pilots

Oregon State Department of Commerce
Corporation Division
158 12th Street, N.E.
Salem, OR 97310
  Investment advisor
  Securities broker-dealer
  Securities salesperson

Oregon State Department of Commerce
Electrical Safety Section
1400 S.W. 5th Avenue
Portland, OR 97201
or
617 Chemeketa
Salem, OR 97310
  Electrical contractors and dealers
  Electrician
  Electrician, limited
  Electrician, limited supervising
  Electrician, supervising
  Elevator safety
  Mobile homes and trailers

Oregon State Department of Commerce
Insurance Division
158 12th Street, N.E.
Salem, OR 97310
- Independent adjustor
- Insurance agent
- Insurance company
- Non-resident broker
- Non-resident insurance agent
- Surplus line agent

Oregon State Board of Cosmetic Therapy
520 State Office Building
Portland, OR 97201
- Cosmetician
- Cosmetician teacher
- Cosmetics demonstrators
- Electrologist
- Guest artist permit
- Beauty school
- Beauty shop
- Teacher trainee

Oregon State Board of Dental Examiners
401 Oregon National Building
Portland, OR 97205
- Dentist
- Dental hygienist

Oregon State Department of Education
942 Lancaster Drive, N.E.
Salem, OR 97310
- Private vocational school
- Teacher

Oregon State Engineer
1178 Chemeketa, N.E.
Salem, OR 97310
- Drilling machine operator
- Water well contractor

Oregon State Board of Engineering Examiners
201 Commerce Building
Salem, OR 97310
- Professional engineer
- Professional land surveyor

Fish Commission of Oregon
307 State Office Building
Portland, OR 97201
- Fish buyer
- Carp permit
- Commercial boat fishing
- Fish canner
- Gill net
- Set net
- Shellfish canner
- Single delivery
- Fish wholesaler

Oregon State Department of Forestry
2600 State Street
Salem, OR
- Notification of forest operations
- Permit to operate power-driven machinery
- Permit to clear right-of-way
- Permit for sawmill construction
- Permit for fires on forest land
- Permit to enter closed area
- Log brand registration;
- Log patrol license
- Easement on state-owned forest land
- Special use permit for non-timber activities on state-owned land
- Log export permit
- Free use permit
- Permit for sale of miscellaneous forest products

Oregon State Board of Funeral Directors and Embalmers
503 State Office Building
Portland, OR 97201
- Embalmer
- Funeral director
- Funeral establishment

Oregon State Game Commission
1634 S.W. Alder Street
Portland, OR 97208
- Fur dealer
- Game breeder
- Guide
- Holding permit
- Hunting and fishing

Private hatcheries
  Private hunting preserve
  Salmon and steelhead tags
  Scientific
  Taxidermist
  Trapper

Oregon State Department of Fish and Wildlife
Portland, OR

  Permit to place explosives or harmful substances in waters (during construction work)
  License for propagation of wildlife including gamefish
  Salmon hatchery permit

Oregon State Department of Geology and Mineral Industries
1400 S.W. 5th
Portland, OR 97201

  Permit to drill stratigraphic test hole
  Permit to drill new oil or gas well
  Permit to drill geophysical test hole
  Permit to drill geothermal well
  Permit for surface mining operation
  Certificate of exemption from surface mining permit

Oregon State Board of Health
Cascade Building
520 S.W. 6th Avenue
Portland, OR 97207

  Apprentice plumber
  Clinical laboratory
  Farm labor camps
  Group care homes
  Hearing aid dealer
  Homes for the aged
  Hospitals
  Massage business
  Masseur or masseuse
  Mobile home and tourist facilities
  Nursing homes
  Nursing home administrator
  Plumber
  Plumbing contractor
  Sewage and cesspools
  Swimming facilities

Oregon State Department of Human Resources
Public Service Building
Salem, OR

Certificate of need for construction or additions to health care facilities
Restaurants
Temporary restaurants
Limited service restaurants
Vending machines
Commissaries
Mobile food and beverage units
Sanitation certificate for tourist facilities
Sanitation certificate for recreation park
Sanitation certificate for organization camp
Furniture and bedding manufacturer
Furniture and bedding upholsterer
Furniture and bedding retailer
Furniture and bedding wholesaler
Furniture and bedding fumigator
Furniture and bedding supplier sanitation certificate
Swimming pool plans approval
Shellfish sanitation certificate for growers, harvesters, shucker-packers, and distributors
Community water supply systems
Packaged food storage warehouses
Child care agencies
Day care centers

Oregon State Board of Higher Education
P.O. Box 3175
Eugene, OR 97403
   Basic science certificate

Oregon State Bureau of Labor
115 Labor and Industries Building
Salem, OR 97310
or
State Office Building
Portland, OR 97201
   Apprenticeship and training
   Employment agencies
   Farm labor contractors

Oregon State Board of Landscape Architect Examiners
1174 Commercial StreeT, S.E.
Salem, OR 97302
   Landscape architects

Oregon State Division of State Lands
   Prospecting permit for minerals on state lands
   Exploratory permit for oil and gas on state lands

Permit for geothermal exploration on state lands
Geothermal lease on state lands
Mining lease on state lands
Oil, gas, and sulphur lease on state lands or tidelands
Treasure trove permit
Permit to remove semi-precious stones from state land
Permit to remove "lost and found" materials valued over $500
Permit for removal of archaeological or historical material from state land
Permit for removal or filling in waters of the state
Royalty lease for removal of materials from state land
Lease for submerged and submersible lands

Oregon Liquor Control Commission
9201 S.E. McLoughlin Boulevard
Portland, OR 97222
   Retail malt beverage
   Package store
   Restaurant beverage
   Health care facility
   Seasonal dispenser
   Dispenser, Class A or B
   Brewery
   Wholesale malt beverage and wine
   Bottler
   Winery
   Farmers' winery
   Distillery
   Manufacture and sale of industrial alcohol
   Rail, passenger carrier, or boat
   Druggist sales
   Import certificate
   Special retail beer
   Special retail wine
   Special dispenser
   Special events dispenser

Oregon State Marine Board
Agriculture Building
Salem, OR 97310
   Undocumented boats

Oregon Medical Examiners
611 Failing Building
Portland, OR 97204
   Osteopathic physician
   Physician

Oregon State Motor Vehicles Division
1905 Lana Avenue, N.E.
Salem, OR 97310
or
5821 N.E. Gilsan Street
Portland, OR 97213
- Campers
- Chauffeurs
- Commercial driver schools
- Dealers
- Motor vehicles
- Operators
- Snowmobiles
- Snowmobile dealers
- Trailers
- Wreckers

Oregon State Board of Naturopathic Examiners
1920 Kilpatrick
Portland, OR 97217
- Naturopathic physicians

Oregon State Board of Nursing
State Office Building
Portland, OR 97201
- Licensed practical nurses
- Registered professional nurses

Oregon State Board of Optometry Examiners
808 S. Main
Milton-Freewater, OR 97862
- Optometrists

Oregon State Board of Pharmacy
State Office Building
Portland, OR 97201
- Itinerant vendor
- Drug manufacturer
- Pharmacist
- Pharmacist intern
- Pharmacy
- Retail shopkeeper for non-prescription drugs
- Wholesaler

Oregon State Physical Therapy Licensing Board
Oregon National Building
Portland, OR 97205
- Physical therapist
- Physical therapist assistant

Oregon State Board of Podiatry Examiners
P.O. Box 231,
Portland, OR 97207
- Podiatrist

Oregon State Board of Psychologist Examiners
P.O. Box 3226
Salem, OR 97302
- Psychologists

Oregon Racing Commission
State Office Building
Portland, OR 97201

Horse Racing
- Apprentice jockey
- Assumed name
- Authorized agent
- Driver training
- Exercise boy
- General
- Groom
- Jockey
- Jockey agent
- Mutuel employee
- Owner
- Plater
- Trainer
- Valet

Greyhound Racing
- Assumed name
- Authorized agent
- General
- Groom
- Mutuel employee
- Owner
- Trainer

Oregon State Department of Commerce
Real Estate Division
Commerce Building
Salem, OR 97310

or
State Office Building
Portland, OR 97201
- Associated real estate brokers
- Assumed business names
- Branch offices
- Broker restricted to appraisal
- Collection agency
- Collection agency operators
- Collection agency solicitors
- Co-partnerships
- Corporation officers
- Debt consolidating agents
- Escrows and escrow agents
- Real estate brokers
- Real estate salespeople
- Subdividers'/developers' notice
- Condominium notice

Sanitarians Registration Board
State Office Building
Portland, OR 97201
- Registered sanitarian
- Sanitarian trainee

Oregon State Television and Radio Service Advisory Board
208 Commerce Building
Salem, OR 97310
- Electronic technician
- Electronic technician trainee
- Service dealer

Oregon State Television and Radio Service Advisory Board
208 Commerce Building
Salem, OR 97310
- Electronic technician
- Electronic technician trainee
- Service dealer

Oregon State Veterinary Examining Board
580 State Street
Salem, OR 97301
- Veterinarian

Oregon State Board of Watchmaking and Clockmaking
209 Commerce Building
Salem, OR 97310

Clockmaker
Watchmaker

Oregon State Water Resources Board
1158 Chemeketa N.E.
Salem, OR 97310
- Hydroelectric projects
- Reservoir construction permit
- Permit to appropriate public waters
- Permit to appropriate ground waters
- Transfer of water rights
- Permit for non-conforming well construction
- Major hydraulic structures
- Irrigation/drainage construction

Oregon State Workers' Compensation Board
Labor and Industries Building
Salem, OR 97310
- Shore-based material handling devices
- Radio systems for logging operations

Oregon State Department of Transportation
Highway Division
Highway Building
Salem, OR 97310
- Permit to construct road approach
- Permit to perform operations on state highway or property
- On premise sign permit
- Permit for development on ocean shore
- Permit for removal of ocean shore products (sand, rock, minerals, marine growth, etc.)
- Permit to change land use within one quarter mile of scenic waterways (Parts of Clackamas, Deschutes, Illinois, John Day, Owyhee, Rogue, and Sandy Rivers and all of Minan River)

Department of Commerce
Building Codes Division
325 13th N.E.
Salem, OR 97310
- Review of plans for fire and life safety
- Building permit and plans review
- Mobile home park plans review and sanitation certificate
- Mechanical permit
- Electrical permit
- Plumbing permit
- Permit for installation of elevator, escalator, or moving walk
- Permit for installation, alteration or repair of boiler or pressure vessel

Boiler or pressure vessel operation
Amusement rides

Oregon State Fire Marshall
688 Church Street, N.E.
Salem, OR 97310
   Existing non-conforming building permit
   Health institution
   Fireworks permits (Public display, retail sales)
   Liquified petroleum gas installers or fitters
   Installation of LPG for use as motor fuel
   Installation of LPG tank
   Operation of LPG equipment mounted on delivery trucks
   Liquified petroleum gas installation
   Permit for installation to handle, store, and distribute flammable liquids
   Possession of explosives

10. Permit coordination center

If all the foregoing seems a little bit too much, take heart! Help is on the way! Recognizing that all this licensing is getting out of hand, the Legislature recently established a permit coordination center where you can take care of a big part of your requirements all at one place. Here you fill out a Master Application answering a broad range of questions about your planned activities. This is circulated to all concerned agencies. If they decide a permit or license is required from their agency, you will be supplied with copies of the necessary application forms. If public hearings are required by more than one agency, you may request a single consolidated hearing.

Now all this may sound easier. Actually you wind up having to fill out one more form and then waiting 30 days before you get all the responses. But it is a step in the right direction and there is hope for more to come. For information on all the permits covered under this program contact:

Permit Coordination Center
Intergovernmental Relations Division
240 Cottage Street, S.E.
Salem, OR 97310
Phone: 378-3732 in Salem or
   1-800-452-0347 (toll free)

7
HOW TO GET FINANCING

Now you have decided to take the plunge and start your own business. However, you need money and you don't have any. Naturally, as with most people, you ask yourself, "How much money do I have to invest?" That is the wrong approach. What you should be thinking is: "Where can I rent money, at reasonable rates of interest, that will allow me to expand, pay back the loan, and still make a profit?"

Now, the first thing to get clear in your mind is that you should never think in terms of "borrowing" money, because the very word "borrowing" is bad for morale. It could create a feeling of inferiority. For too many people, the word "borrowing" leaves a bad taste in the mouth. Why should you, a self-made business person, harbor a sense of failure, just because you know it is wiser and safer to use somebody else's money rather than your own?

For example, if you are taking a holiday, and you and your family rent a boat for a day or a week, does that feel like "borrowing"? Of course not! In reality you are doing the marina a favor. They earn their living by "renting" boats and motors. If you rent an apartment suite in a fancy new high-rise building, do you feel "cheap" because you are renting? Hardly. You know full well that the people who built the apartment complex in the first place made the investment so that they could rent luxury suites at a good profit.

So, why feel "bad" about renting money, especially when you rent only from people who need your business? Firms such as banks, finance companies, and other "money rental" operators need your business in order to justify their existence!

You can create a lucrative business and be independent fast, using "rented" money to get started. And why not? "Renting" money is a sound and recognized way to do business. Therefore, starting now, get used to the idea, and "rent" money the same way you would rent a car, boat, or summer cottage. Money is just another commodity, the same as a boat or a car, so use the "money rental system" to become financially independent.

Let's get something straight right away. Never "rent" money just for the sake of having a few bucks in your jeans. That's plain stupid. You should rent money only when you have a definite and sound money-making plan whereby you can use some other person's cash to build yourself a tidy fortune. And you, as a sound business person, need money to expand your business. So, let's get started in the game of "renting" money to make money for yourself.

How do you go about doing this? Well, there are actually many places to go, almost too numerous to mention. However, you must do your homework first. By this, I mean you've got to have a precise plan worked out, in full detail, before you ever approach anyone for money.

There are thousands of different ways to earn a living in this country of ours. And when you come right down to it, each type of business has its own specialized methods and sources of financing (or so it seems). The point is, there are so many types of businesses that financial institutions tend to specialize in certain types. Your problem, then, is to find that one institution that specializes in your type of business.

a. BE PRACTICAL AND REALISTIC

Now, here's where doing your homework is important. When you find that right money source, you're going to find yourself dealing with people who are probably very familiar with the type of business you are proposing to go into. If you don't have all your facts straight, they'll spot them in a minute. This won't necessarily rule you out. But it does make them wonder just how capable you are.

Part of this homework will involve coming down to the most reasonable amount of money to ask for. Many people go into business expecting to become millionaires overnight. Now, there's nothing wrong with having this kind of a goal. In fact, it's the very essence of our American capitalistic system. However, don't expect anyone to do you any favors getting there.

What I'm getting at is this. If, up to now, you've only been earning $5,000 a year, or $10,000, or even $25,000, don't expect anyone to put up money for a business where you'll earn fabulous profits during the first year. You can get there, but you have to work your way up to it. This applies, even if you are an inventor.

I've had occasion to work with a number of inventors. Many of them have had great ideas for new products; they even had patents on them. Somehow, getting a patent gives some inventors the idea that they have the world by the tail. They become convinced that they are bound to make a million dollars and don't need to share it with anyone. After all, didn't they do all the work in making the invention? Don't they deserve the rewards?

The answer is "No." Why? Well, you see, in issuing a patent, the patent office is only acknowledging that the inventor had a certain idea first and is giving rights for its use for a certain period of time. It has done nothing to investigate the practicality of the idea, its market potential, or the potential hazards and liabilities that may occur with its use.

So, it becomes the responsibility of the person putting up the money to check into these aspects of making a certain new product. The inventor only puts up an idea; the investor puts up the hard cash and takes all the risks. Now, who do you think should get the major share of the profits of that enterprise?

Partially understanding this, some inventors come up with very magnanimous offers. They'll form a corporation, assign their patent rights to it, and let the investors putting up all the money have 49% of the stock. All they want is 51% of the stock, just enough to retain control of the business. I'm sorry to say that even this is seldom good enough. Those investors putting up their hard-earned cash have no guarantee that the inventor knows anything about managing a business. Unless the inventor has experience in this capacity with some other company, it's a real gamble for them.

"No," as I said earlier, "don't expect anyone to do you any favors." If you have a red hot idea that is bound to make a million the first year, great! Such ideas eventually find someone to finance them. But be willing to accept something more like 10% to 25% ownership of the business for your idea. You may even be able to start out managing the business. If you do a good job, you'll be able to keep that role. But if you don't do a good job, the investors will have to make a change to protect their investment. In the process, they will be protecting and enhancing your share of the business too! Either way, you win!

Some inventors struggle on year after year on minimal incomes rather than accept partial ownership of what could easily be multi-million dollar-a-year businesses. I knew one inventor who held out right to his dying day. Now his invention, which would have been a real boon to the handicapped, will never be made.

Well, I've taken a long time to get to my point. You must be realistic in your expectations. You must tailor your initial financial requirements to what an investor or banker can reasonably agree with. Finally, you must make a good first impression. You can do this in three ways:

(a) by dressing appropriately
(b) by projecting a positive image and
(c) by being thoroughly prepared with a detailed presentation.

b. MAKING A GOOD IMPRESSION

Let's talk about appropriate dress and grooming. I'm not saying you always have to wear a suit, although it would probably never hurt your chances. What I am saying is that you should dress at least as well as you would have to for the business you want to start.

In other words, if you're going to wind up as a white collar worker, then wear a business suit or a conservative, but attractive, dress or suit if you are a woman. However, if you are planning to open an auto repair shop, for instance, you can dress more casually. But don't show up in greasy overalls either!

These days, it's hard to say much about grooming. Long hair, beards, and pantsuits are obviously acceptable within certain limits. Just remember that investors tend to be conservative people in their action and in their tastes. Enough said on that!

How do you project a positive image? Whole books have been written on this subject. I couldn't begin to do justice to it in this book. My whole reason for bringing up the subject is this: you must understand that the investors or bankers are looking you over as a potential partner. They are trying to decide how well they'd like to be working with you, how well you would manage employees, how well you would handle customers, and most of all, how well you're going to try to make money for them.

So, you need to go in there looking as though you are in full command of the situation. Don't go in with hat in hand, looking as though you are asking for a hand-out. Look them squarely in the eye, smile, and talk to them as if you're going to do them a favor. After all, you really are. You're going to help them make more money.

Keep the conversation in a very positive tone. Don't get off on a discussion on how bad the economy is. Instead, point out the bright spots. Maybe new car sales have really nose-dived. Okay, so you are planning on opening an auto repair shop. Then point out how car-repair work is bound to increase, as people try to squeeze an extra year or two out of their old car. Show them that you can lead the conversation through a few pleasantries, into a brief sales pitch, and finally into the heart of the matter — your detailed presentation.

c. HAVE A PREPARED PLAN ON PAPER

This brings me to the final point in making a good impression. That is, you have to have a well-prepared business plan. Talking in generalities just won't do! You've got to have it on paper. Put certain basic information in an attractive package, neatly typed. If you aren't too sharp on spelling and grammar, have someone help you. Similarly, if you aren't too sharp on math, find someone to help you there. Provide photographs where possible. Remember, a picture is still worth a thousand words. Show originality wherever you can.

One word of caution — don't overdo it! Your presentation should be long enough to give the investor all the pertinent information, but not so long that he or she loses interest in it.

To avoid this problem, always provide a one-page summary right at the beginning, with the basic facts you want to emphasize. Remember, most investors see many proposals every day. You want yours to stand out from the crowd.

Here is a sample of a detailed presentation. it will apply equally well to a new idea or to cases of expansion. Just one comment: use 8-1/2 inch by 11 inch sheets. They are easiest to have photocopied, and most people's files are set up to handle that size.

SAMPLE #1
BUSINESS PLAN

First page:

This page will be primarily a cover sheet, so it should only have a brief title and explanation, such as:

An Invitation to Invest
in
A B C Company
123 Fourth Street
Portland, OR 97201
Telephone: (503) 123-4567

for the purpose of establishing a new manufacturing plant in Oregon to produce widgets.

Section I: BACKGROUND INFORMATION

Under this section, outline the history of your company: when started, where started, general type of business, highlights of growth, record of earnings, current data on size of company (including number of employees), gross sales for previous year, net income (or loss) for previous year, location of manufacturing plants, warehouses, sales offices, etc. A few pictures of main facilities would be helpful.

If you are establishing a new company, give a history of the development of the product or the idea, including information on any patents you may have.

This section should not exceed three pages in length.

Section II: MANAGEMENT

Give the following information on all the key members of your management team. (**Note:** It is important to have well-qualified persons lined up to handle all phases of your business — sales, production, engineering, financial controller, etc.)

Name, title, age, education, length of service with company, previous experience by years in type of industry and level of responsibility. Small photographs would be appropriate if available.

This section should not be more than two pages in length.

Section III: DESCRIPTION OF NEW VENTURE

Under this section, describe what you want to do, how you propose to do it, and how much it's going to cost (total only). Mention the type of product, planned production rate, type of facility required, type of equipment required, estimated time to get into full operation, raw materials required, special utilities required, and number of employees required.

This section should not be more than three pages in length.

Section IV: DESCRIPTION OF PRODUCT

Provide the information a potential customer needs, including: general description, specifications, possible variations, comparison with similar products currently on the market, pictures if available, and estimated selling price.

This section should not be more than three pages in length.

Section V: MARKET ANALYSIS

Provide whatever information you have been able to gather that will give an indication of the potential quantities you can expect to sell. This should include: the total market, the location of the market, the percentage you hope to capture, the nature of the market (seasonal, expanding, etc.), some idea of the uniqueness of your product, or the need for your product. Try to establish the reliability of your information, wherever possible.

This section should not be more than three pages in length.

Section VI: FINANCIAL STATEMENT

This should be a standard itemization of assets in one column and liabilities in another column. Both columns should be totalled, and the difference shown as net worth. In addition to this, it would be well to report the ratio of your current liabilities to current assets. If you are an individual starting a new company, it will be necessary to prepare the same information on your personal net worth. If at all possible, this should be audited.

This information should be on one page. A separate page for an auditor's comments may be included.

Section VII: PROJECTED OPERATING STATEMENT FOR NEW VENTURE

This should be a detailed itemization of your total operating costs on a quarterly basis for at least a three-year period, showing such items as labor, materials, supervision, utilities, rent, depreciation, taxes, insurance, advertising, maintenance costs, distribution costs, construction costs, administrative costs, etc. This should be followed with a detailed itemization of quarterly income including sales, royalties, sale of stock, and proceeds from this investment.

The difference between the operating costs and income should be reported as estimated net income. In the final quarter shown, this amount must be sufficient to show the ability to repay the investor on whatever terms are agreed on.

A sample form for this statement is attached.

Section VIII: PROPOSED DISTRIBUTION OF INVESTED FUNDS

This should show as detailed a breakdown as possible of how the funds you are seeking will be used. This may include development costs, purchase of land, construction of buildings, purchase and installation of equipment, administrative costs, and working capital.

If a long time-period is involved, it would be well to indicate your cash flow requirements for the funds requested.

This information should not exceed one page.

Section IX: PROPOSED INVESTMENT CONTRACT

Under this section, you should outline specifically how much funds you need, what form of security you are offering (i.e., shares of stock, percentage of ownership, debenture note, chattel mortgage, etc.) and what form of repayment is proposed. Alternatives may be shown. This section should be signed by a responsible officer or the individual initiating a new company.

This section should also not exceed one page.

SAMPLE #2
PROJECTED OPERATING STATE

Make one for each year for at least three years. (Some investors like to see one for five years.)

A B C COMPANY
Projected Operating Statement
First Year of Operation

Item	1st Quarter	2nd Quarter	3rd Quarter	4th Quarter
Materials and supplies				
Direct labor				
Supervision				
Utilities				
Rent				
Depreciation				
Insurance				
Advertising and sales costs				
Maintenance costs				
Distribution costs				
Construction costs				
Administrative overhead				
State and local taxes				
TOTAL EXPENSES				
Sales				
Royalties				
Sale of stock				
Loans				
TOTAL INCOME				
PROFIT (LOSS) BEFORE TAXES				
FEDERAL INCOME TAX				
NET PROFIT				

8
WHERE TO GET FINANCING

It seems that each type of business has its own appropriate forms and sources of financing. Probably 90% of new businesses fall into the category of a retail or service-oriented business serving the local community. Obviously, the source of financing for this type of business will normally be the conventional financial sources within the community. So, let's start with those, and then go on to the more specialized sources.

a. BANKS

The most obvious source of financing is your local bank, preferably the one you've been dealing with all along. If you've established yourself with that local branch over a period of years, you will have a better leverage there than anywhere else. Hopefully, you've shown an ability to keep your financial affairs in order. By managing your checking account without an overdraft for a number of years, you've already proven to the bank that you are reliable and reputable. Furthermore, they know that if they refuse a reasonable request for a loan, they stand a good chance of losing a valued customer.

One word of advice: the name of the bank is irrelevant. It's the manager you want to know and stick with no matter where he/she goes (within reason, of course). Find a good manager, and you've got it made. To find one, ask other business people in your position, friends, and your accountant. Keep looking until you find the one for you. It is important that you find someone who is responsive to your needs.

Bank loans can take a variety of forms:

1. Unsecured loans

The easiest type of loan to arrange is a personal loan — and a personal loan can be used for practically anything. Granted, the interest rate may be higher, but it will still be cheaper than alternative sources.

On your first loan, the interest should not worry you too much, especially if you are renting from a bank, because a bank's interest rate is controlled and not expensive. However, rented money should be put in savings until actually needed to offset the total cost of that rented money. And don't forget that all interest you pay on borrowed money is deductible for income tax purposes. Remember that when starting out in your own business. Personal loans are the quickest way to rent needed capital.

Also, the *bigger* your present income, the *larger* the loan you can arrange. So, when applying for a loan, always list *every* source of possible income that you have, including wages, interest earned, stocks, insurance, spouse's income, rental income — everything.

Regrettably, some banks have a well-deserved reputation for being prepared to advance money for a personal loan while, at the same time, refusing to consider a business loan. (They make more money on a "consumer" loan.) I have heard of several cases of banks turning down loans to small business persons for legitimate requests for working capital, then turning around and lending cash to the same people for a trip to Hawaii or to buy a new car.

If you find your request for a business loan being repeatedly turned down (shop around, remember), then you may be forced to cheat the system by asking for a personal loan when, in fact, you need it for that new business. I leave it to each individual in this situation to work out the ethics of the situation.

2. Co-signed loans

A co-signer is a person who is willing to sign your loan application, promising to repay the loan if you default on your promise. Having a co-signer makes it easier to get a personal loan, especially if your present income is low or if your past repayment history leaves much to be desired. Bankers feel much more secure when they have two or more signatures on a loan application.

A co-signer's income is often more important to the lender than your own, because the lender must feel certain that the co-signer earns enough money to pay back the loan in the event that you don't. You can use a friend, relative, or your spouse as co-signer, provided that he or she has a source of income.

Is it dishonest to hire someone to be a co-signer? No. If someone you know wants to be paid to be a co-signer, then you may have to do so in order to get that loan. If this is the case, then you just have to be practical and businesslike, and pay for services rendered.

3. Accounts receivable loans

One of the big problems in many new businesses is having enough funds to extend credit to their customers. Obviously, the first solution is to try to work on a "cash only" basis. Yet, competing effectively in many types of business almost dictates that you operate on a monthly billing basis. Your bank can help out here. They can extend loans or a line of credit based on a certain percentage of your outstanding accounts receivable.

4. Floor plan loans

Suppose you plan to set up a place to sell automobiles or large home appliances? The cost of your inventory can be substantial, in this case. Again, your bank can help out. It can put up the money for each of your inventory purchases. Such loans are then repaid immediately upon sale of that particular item. These plans are usually combined with an arrangement, whereby the bank takes over installment contracts at a discount.

5. Purchase of installment accounts

Any business dealing in expensive items must have some arrangement for selling on an installment basis. One way this can be done is to make arrangements for the bank to take over any accounts established at a discount.

6. Bank credit cards

One of the more popular means of extending credit to customers is the use of one or more of the bank credit cards. Getting approval to use this sytem is probably easiest of all, because the bank is concerned with the card holder's credit, not yours.

7. Inventory loans

For products other than durable goods, arrangements other than floor plan loans must be made to cover inventory costs. Such goods rarely allow individual item accounting. Therefore, the bank will come to some agreement to loan a percentage of the average inventory.

8. Chattel mortgages on equipment

Buying new equipment can be a major expense to a new business. Banks can help out here, by loaning money to purchase the equipment in return for a chattel mortgage as security.

9. Construction loans

For those of you going into the construction contracting field, this form of financing will almost certainly be necessary. Under this type of loan, the bank provides sufficient funds to cover labor and materials expenses during the construction phase. As soon as the house or building is sold, the loan is repaid. Initially, you will probably find the bank withholding payments, until they have satisfied themselves that a reasonable percentage of work has been completed. Be patient! Once they get to know your work, they will probably be fairly easy to deal with.

10. Other secured loans

You may find that you have other assets, either personal or belonging to your business, that would serve as collateral for a loan. This could include such things as: your home (whether it is mortgaged or not), real estate contracts, life insurance, marketable securities, purchase orders on hand, contracts for your services, and letters of agreement.

b. PERSONAL SOURCES

While potentially the most attractive, because of the low or even non-existent interest and flexible payback schedule, personal friends and rich uncles or aunts should be avoided, if possible. Probably the reason your rich uncle will cough up is because he likes you personally. Nevertheless, you are running a business, and money lent on any other basis should not have been lent in the first place. Also, if you have such a sound, money-making idea, why won't the bank or credit union lend you what you want?

If, by chance, you have someone who is dying to put some money into your little enterprise, or you simply cannot turn down the chance for cheap, easy money, make sure it is all done on a proper, businesslike level, with the proper security, interest payments, etc. If you cannot avoid the personal involvement, at least you can cut down the risk of personal problems.

c. WHAT ABOUT SELLING SOME OF THE EQUITY?

In a brand new business there is usually little, if any, equity value, but you may interest someone in buying a share in the "potential equity" of your business — which is speculating rather than anything else. First, let's be clear about what the term "equity capital" means. There are many definitions, but the simplest is that *the equity in any business is that part of the money invested in it which is not debt.*

1. The advantages of using equity capital

By using equity capital you will be able:
- (a) To expand the borrowing power of the company (a larger equity base permits this)
- (b) To improve the company's credit rating with its suppliers
- (c) To reduce the risk to each owner of the business
- (d) To spread the ownership of the company over more shareholders who may be more venturesome than if only a few owners were involved

(e) To gain the experience and counsel of new shareholders

Your company should always raise additional equity before the need for it becomes urgent. If the search for new investors is delayed until all other sources have been exhausted, bargaining power is weakened, and new capital may be available only on onerous terms to you, the owner.

2. The disadvantages of using equity capital

Using equity capital, however, can also mean:

(a) A possible lessening of flexibility because of shared ownership

(b) The dilution of ownership interest of the original owners

(c) Possible increased expenses, such as costs incurred in issuing the stock, dividend payments, and accounting

Remember, as the sole owner of a business, you enjoy complete flexibility of operating and complete power in the decision-making process. You do not need to consult anyone; you can take risks that a financial partner may not wish to share. In short, you are your own boss, whereas the sale of stock to new investors is really the same as admitting new partners to the business. The owner now has to share control with others. In effect, you probably become an employee of the company's owners, of whom you are one.

In addition, selling partial ownership in a business by introducing new investors reduces your share in the company's profits. On the other hand, the refusal to sell additional shares could impair the growth of the business or allow competitors to overtake it.

Conversely, the premature sale of stock in a growth company could subsequently make the original owner reluctant to reduce his or her ownership interest further, even though the new funding was vitally needed.

The sale of a portion of the equity usually involves additional expenses. Legal fees may be involved. The business's accounting system will probably have to be expanded for the protection and information of the new investor co-owners. Furthermore, a more disciplined standard of conduct may be forced on you, when you reduce your share of the ownership by selling part of it to others.

3. Sources of equity capital for small companies

Under the free-enterprise system, the basic law of supply and demand applies to the issuance of the securities of any company, large or small. Just as the business's products or services have to be attractive to create and retain customers, so do the securities offered to new investors.

Share offerings of small, relatively unknown companies are often not attractive to the "ordinary" investor, because stability and a regular pattern of profit have yet to be established. However, such securities often prove attractive to those in high tax brackets who may be more interested in the prospect of capital gains, than in increasing their incomes further through a stable dividend payment pattern.

Small businesses rarely have access to a public offering. Investment dealers and underwriting houses have necessarily to be convinced of the marketability of a proposed public offering among their clientele. Furthermore, the cost of placing a small issue for a small company is usually disproportionate to the net yield to it in new equity funding. So, the small company that wants to become bigger by increasing its share capitalization will probably first seek private sources of equity capital.

(a) Private sources

Internal sources of equity capital would comprise additional investment by the present owners and, perhaps, the sale of shares to employees of the company — a form of employee profit-sharing.

External sources for a small company would include relatives and friends of the owner, and even customers and suppliers. The latter two possible sources may, however, result in undue restrictions on the company's operations, and could induce reluctance by other customers and suppliers to deal with it. Often, a single professional investor or group operating as a syndicate will provide equity capital directly to a small business, if the prospect appears unusually attractive. The best place to find such people is to make inquiries through your bank manager, accounting firm, or a lawyer who has contacts in this area.

(b) Non-private sources

Non-private sources do not include a public stock issue, for the reasons given earlier. Similarly, mutual funds usually confine their investment portfolios to large, well-established, and well-known companies. However, the small company can turn to several non-private sources of equity capital, one of which is often overlooked — other companies.

Larger companies are quite often willing to invest in smaller ones, not necessarily to the point of taking them over completely, but limiting their share interest to some maximum percentage of ownership, which is often less than sufficient to acquire control. The reasons for larger companies doing this would include the desire to retain contact with an individual or to buy an interest in a development pattern in a field in which they were not active themselves. Alternatively, the operations of the larger and of the smaller company may complement each other, and the case of a large company acquiring a smaller competitor is, of course, frequently encountered.

In seeking this type of equity source, you should be sure that you seek the services of an intermediary — a person whose business judgment you trust. As suggested earlier, your banker and accountant would be good people to start with.

As a final possibility, there is an increasing number of venture capital firms which you might consider. Often, they are owned by a consortium of banks, trust companies, and other pools of capital. They specialize in investing in small companies seen to have strong growth potential through good management and product acceptance — especially a high technology product.

d. EQUITY CAPITAL SOURCES HERE IN THE NORTHWEST

1. Small Business Investment Corporations (SBIC)

These are a special type of investment company licensed under federal legislation giving them certain tax advantages and making federal loans available to them. They are specifically designed to provide small businesses with long-term capital. Loans must be made to firms not dominant in their field of operation. Investments by an SBIC can take several forms:

(a) Long-term loans secured by appropriate collateral
(b) Purchase of convertible debentures
(c) Purchase of preferred or common stock

Such firms serving the Pacific Northwest include:

Cascade Capital Corporation
421 S.W. Sixth
Portland, Oregon

Capital Investors Corporation
Dexter Horton Building
Seattle, Washington 98104

Endeavor Capital Corporation
310 Oregon Street, N.E.
Portland, Oregon

Future Capital Corporation
4218 Roosevelt Way, N.E.
Seattle, Washington 98105

Northwest Capital Investment Corporation
315 Holton Avenue
Yakima, Washington 98901

Northwest Business Investment Corporation
929 Sprague Avenue
Spokane, Washington 98204

Oregon Small Business Investment Corporation
661 High Street, N.E.
Salem, Oregon

Model Capital Corporation
105 14th Avenue
Seattle, Washington 98122

Small Business Investment Co. of America
1711 IBM Building
Seattle, Washington 98154

The San Francisco-Pacific Fund
807 International Building
Portland, Oregon 97205

Washington Capital Corporation
1417 Fourth Avenue
Seattle, Washington

Western Venture Resources, Inc.
3734 Seattle First National Bank Building
Seattle, Washington 98154

2. Local Development Companies (LDC's)

Many communities throughout the state have established non-profit organizations to assist in the economic growth of the community. Usually, they are set up to provide a small portion of the total amount that is required along with a Small Business Administration loan. However, they frequently play a far more important part in establishing a good working relationship with the local business community. Such companies include:

Astoria Industrial Development Corporation
270 — 14th
Astoria 97103

Baker Industrial Development Corporation
2015 Main
Baker 97814

Bend Industrial Development Corporation
1037 Brooks Street
Bend 97701

Brookings Development Corporation
1417 Parkview Drive
Brookings 97415

Central Curry Development Corporation
P.O. Box 517
Gold Beach 97444

Cottage Grove Development Corporation
634 Jefferson Street
Cottage Grove 97424

East Linn Development Corporation
P.O. Box 486
Sweet Home 97386

Eugene Industrial Development Corporation
230 East Broadway
Eugene 97401

Forest Grove Development, Inc.
1933 — 21st Avenue
Forest Grove 97116

Greater Klamath Development Corporation
323 Main Street
Klamath Falls 97601

Hermiston Development Corporation
680 Hermiston Avenue
Hermiston 97838

Hillsboro Industrial Development Corporation
174 East Main Street
Hillsboro 97123

Hood River Improvement Corporation
P.O. Box 60
Hood River 97031

Industries Development, Inc.
c/o First National Bank
Grants Pass 97526

Jefferson County Development Corporation
406 Fifth
Madras 97741

Jobs and Industry, Inc. of Southwest Oregon
P.O. Box 359
Coos Bay 97420

LaGrande Industrial Development Corporation
1402 Adams Avenue
LaGrande 97850

Lebanon Industrial Development Corporation
75 East Oak Street
Lebanon 97355

Lincoln Development Corporation
155 East Olive Street
Newport 97365

Madras Development Corporation
City Hall
Madras 97741

The Mid-Columbia Development Corporation
P.O. Box 84
The Dalles 97058

Milton-Freewater Development Corporation
610-1/2 N. Main Street
Milton-Freewater

Newberg Industrial Development Corporation
700 E. First
Newberg 97132

Nyassa Industries, Inc.
105 Main
Nyassa 97913

Ontario Industries, Inc.
125 South Oregon Street
Ontario 97914

Pendleton Development Corporation
116 S.E. Second Street
Pendleton 97801

Phoenix Development Corporation
4149 South Pacific Highway
Phoenix 97535

Salem Industrial Development Corporation
220 Cottage Street, N.E.
Salem 97308

Santa Clara Development Corporation
36 Irving
Eugene 97402

Santiam Valley Promotion Corporation
P.O. Box 128
Lyons 97358

Shermina Industrial Promotions, Inc.
142 South Bridge Street
Sheridan 97378

Siuslaw Valley Development Corporation
P.O. Box 575
Florence 97439

Space Age Industrial Development Corporation
411 Main
Hermiston 97838

Sutherlin-Oakland Development Corporation
P.O. Box 459
Sutherlin 97479

Umatilla County Development Corporation
P.O. Box 1107
Pendleton 97801

Umatilla Development Corporation
Umatilla 97882

Umpqua Development Corporation
410 S.E. Spruce
Roseburg 97470

Vernonia Industrial Development Corporation
636 Bridge
Vernonia 97064

Woodburn Development Corporation
143 Grant Street
Woodburn 97071

Yamhill Industrial Development Corporation
P.O. Box 278
Yamhill 97148

e. FEDERAL SOURCES

1. Small Business Administration

In 1953, Congress established this independent agency to assist small businesses. For those firms qualifying as a small business, SBA has several funding programs. Loans can be used for business construction, expansion, or conversion, purchase of machinery, equipment, supplies, or materials, and working capital. The Small Business Administration maintains offices at:

700 Pittock Building
921 S.W. Washington Street
Portland, OR 97205

(a) Direct loans

Although funds are limited, SBA is authorized to make direct loans of up to $100,000. With participation by a local bank, this can be increased to $150,000. Unfortunately, interest rates are very restrictive, so few banks are interested in participating in such loans.

(b) Loan guarantee

The most common arrangement is to have SBA guarantee up to 90% or $350,000 whichever is less, of a percent loan from some regular financial institution. The maximum interest rate is 8-1/4%.

(c) Pool loans

Groups of small businesses can form corporations to purchase raw materials, equipment, inventory, or supplies for use by the individual businesses. Such corporations are eligible for loans of up to $250,000 for each pool member. These loans can also be used for conducting research and development.

(d) Economic opportunity loans

This is a special program for the disadvantaged who want to own their own business. Either new or existing busi-

nesses can qualify for up to $25,000 for up to 15 years if one of the following conditions exist:
  (i) The applicant's total family income from all sources, other than welfare, is insufficient to meet the basic needs of the family.
  (ii) The applicant has been denied the chance to obtain adequate financing because of a social or economic disadvantage.

(e) Lease guarantee program
The newest program available through SBA is an insurance, guaranteeing the landlord that rent payments will be made. Two conditions must be made:
  (i) There must be a landlord-tenant relationship with a true lease agreement.
  (ii) Only land and buildings can be covered.

(f) Surety bond guarantee program
Any business required to post a bond to obtain a contract for construction, maintenance, or service supply, is eligible for this program if its annual gross volume of work has been under $750,000 per year. SBA will guarantee 90% of the loss on a bond up to $500,000.

(g) Disaster loans
SBA can make low-interest loans to businesses damaged in disasters. These can be used for repairs, for assistance in overcoming economic injury, for product disasters, and to assist displaced businesses.

2. Economic Development Administration (EDA)
Congress established this agency in 1965 to assist economically distressed areas to rebuild stable and diversified local economies. Most of their efforts are aimed at public works projects in these areas. However, loans are also made for commercial and industrial facilities. EDA can only make loans on the plant and equipment, not working capital. There are no statutory limits on these loans. As a

matter of policy, loans under $350,000 are seldom considered, because these are available from the Small Business Administration. EDA maintains offices at 1220 S.W. Third Street in Portland.

3. Farmers Home Administration (FmHA)

You may wonder how an agency with a name like this gets involved with business loans. Actually, it's very simple. This agency is responsible for rural development. So, business and industry loan guarantees are available from FmHA for any business planning on locating in a community with a population of less than 50,000. Priority is given to communities under 25,000. Loans can be used for plant, equipment, and working capital. FmHA also maintains offices at 1220 S.W. Third Street in Portland.

4. Programs for minority enterprises

The federal government has created a number of programs to assist members of minorities in starting a new business. These include:

Economic opportunity nonfarm enterprise loans
Farmers Home Administration

Farm ownership and farm operating loans
Farmers Home Administration

Indian revolving loan fund
Bureau of Indian Affairs

Minerals discovery loan program
U.S. Geological Survey

Deposit of U.S. government funds in minority banks
Treasury Department

Opportunity funding corporation guaranteed loans, bonds
Office of Economic Opportunity

Operation Business Mainstream — regular business loans 7A
Small Business Administration

f. FACTORING

Factoring is a system whereby the financial institution assumes the credit and collection functions of your business. Firms in this type of business will purchase your receivables as they arise and assume responsibility for any credit losses. A commission is charged to cover the cost of credit, collection, and bad debts. Such firms serving Northwest businesses include:

Walter Heller & Co.
421 S.W. Sixth
Portland, Oregon

Barnett Financial Corp.
2633 Eastlake E.
Seattle, Washington

Manufacturers Acceptance Corporation
W. 104 Mission
Spokane, Washington

Brenek Investments
Tower Building
Seattle, Washington

Guthrie Investment Inc.
N. 1520 Vercier Rd.
Spokane, Washington

Business Factors, Inc.
10 Harrison
Seattle, Washington

g. INSURANCE COMPANIES

Did you ever wonder what insurance companies do with all those millions of dollars in premiums that they receive every year? Sure, they pay out a lot of claims, but they also have to maintain a sizeable reserve. These funds have to be invested until they're needed. Most insurance firms are primarily interested in real estate or blue chip stocks. Many will invest in commercial or industrial real estate, and some will consider investing a certain portion in regular business loans. This is normally handled as a private placement of corporate bonds.

There are a number of Northwest-based insurance companies to talk with. These would be the easiest ones to approach first. However, don't overlook checking with your own insurance agent to find out who handles investments for his or her company.

h. PENSION FUNDS

Everything I mentioned about insurance companies applies even more to any pension fund. If you currently belong to a union having a pension fund, check into this as a possible source of a loan. Some unions have begun to realize it is in their own best interest to assist businesses within their particular industry to create additional jobs.

i. INVESTMENT BROKERS

One of the advantages of incorporating is that you are able to sell securities publicly. However, this is very involved and is governed by the federal Securities Exchange Commission and state securities regulations. Issues of $300,000 or less are classified as Regulation A issues, and have one set of regulations. Issues over that are classified as Regulation C, with another set of more complex regulations. Your best bet for marketing such issues is an investment securities broker, who is completely knowledgeable in these matters. In Oregon such firms include:

Atkinson and Company
720 S.W. Washington
Portland

Black and Company
621 S.W. Morrison
Portland

Blakely, Strand and Williams, Inc.
Commonwealth Building
Portland

Blyth, Eastman, Dillon and Co., Inc.
1300 S.W. Fifth
Portland

Calise and Alexander, Inc.
397 No. State
Lake Oswego

Dean Witter and Company, Inc.
1100 S.W. Sixth
Portland

Foster and Marshall, Inc.
521 S.W. Stark
Portland

Harris Upham and Company, Inc.
200 Market Building
Portland

Herron Northwest
900 S.W. Fifth
Portland

Hinkle Northwest
Georgia Pacific Building
Portland

Paulson Investment Company
729 S.W. Alder
Portland

Merrill, Lynch, Pierce, Fenner, and Smith, Inc.
900 S.W. Fifth
Portland

Saunders Investment Company
415 No. State
Lake Oswego

T.E. Slanker Company
620 S.W. Alder
Portland

Waddel and Reed, Inc.
5319 S.W. Westgate Drive
Portland

j. EQUIPMENT-LEASING COMPANIES

Instead of incurring debts or selling equity in order to finance equipment that you may need, consider leasing that equipment for a few years. Usually, you can get an option to renew the lease at reduced rates at the end of the lease, or to purchase it as used equipment. Another big advantage is that such lease payments are tax deductible where you would have to depreciate straight purchases over a period of years.

This form of financing has become increasingly popular over the past decade. There are currently numerous leasing firms located in most larger cities in the state. Check in the Yellow Pages for firms near you.

k. PORT DISTRICTS

Port districts are one of the primary industrial development agencies throughout the state. As such, they are authorized to provide financing to new or expanding companies, using tax exempt industrial revenue bonds. These can be used to acquire land, construct manufacturing facilities, and buy capital equipment.

The port actually buys and constructs the desired facilities and then leases or sells them to the company. Since the bonds offer the investor tax-free interest income, the interest rate that the port district has to pay is significantly lower. These savings are passed on to the company. Ports are allowed to finance 100% of a project up to a federal limitation of $5,000,000.

l. OTHER SOURCES OF FUNDS

There are still a few other ways of raising money that we haven't discussed. You can incorporate and sell stock by private placement to personal acquaintances. Otherwise, you can just take on a partner who can supply needed capital. Possibly, you can arrange advance payments on orders or contracts from customers. Another possibility is to obtain credit from major suppliers. If you have incorporated, you can also sell debenture bonds.

Many private parties are interested in making business investments. Getting in touch with these investors is very unorganized. Occasionally, they will place ads in the classified ads of major newspapers under some heading, such as "Money to Loan."

SAMPLE

```
525 Money to Loan
        MONEY TO LOAN!
  1— We buy or loan on Real Estate
     contracts
  2—We loan on home equity or on
     real estate for any reason.
  3—Consolidation of debts
  4—Home improvements
  5—Business capital
     ASK FOR BILL, 682-4950
        VENTURE CAPITAL
                and
         FINANCING AVAILABLE
      FOR TROUBLED COMPANIES
  623-1532              622-0297
  BUSINESS LOANS. $10,000 or
  more. Also 1st & 2nd mortgages
  $6,000 to $100,000,000. Call Donald
  Supernor, 827-7321.

  BUSINESS, Industrial & individual
  loans, any purpose $2000$25,-
  000,000. J.W. Kennedy 363-8911
  WHEN banks say no, we say go:
     Projects over 50K 1- 627-3215
```

They often let their bankers know that they are interested in certain types of investments. The trick, then, is to get in touch with the right banker. There are also a number of financial consultants around who specialize in finding these private investors. Some of these are completely reputable, others are not. If you go to one of these, be prepared to sign a contract to pay a certain percentage of whatever amount of money is obtained. Be very cautious about making any advance payments or tying yourself to an exclusive contract, where the consultant receives a finder's fee, regardless of where you ultimately receive your financing from.

9

WHAT TO DO WHEN YOU ARE SHORT OF CASH*

One of the most common complaints of any small business owner is: "Why am I always short of cash?" Usually there are two basic reasons. The first revolves around the owner's expectations of business growth, etc. (especially in an inflationary period). Because there is a need to be positive about the future of the business and all its aspects, the owner tends to be overly optimistic about how much money is coming in and how much is needed from outside sources. Projections of reaching the break-even point in a year can easily stretch on to eighteen months of two years.

The second reason is that the average small business owner frequently does not have time to pay proper attention to the state of his or her accounts and to the handling of payables. Closing that big sale or simply meeting next week's payroll seems more important. The only problem is that the people owing you money will sense this and tend to drag out paying *your* account (as opposed to your bigger, somewhat better-organized competitor).

The purpose of this chapter is to outline several methods for maximizing internal cash flow.

Taken individually, the various points may not seem to be earth shattering. They're not. Put together, however, the eight suggestions can make the difference between a cash-strapped firm and one which rolls along smoothly on cash-greased wheels.

---

*Parts of this chapter are printed from an article entitled "How to Build up Your Cash Position" appearing in the August 1976 edition of the *C.G.A. Magazine* with thanks to Claude A. Tomas and the *C.G.A. Magazine*.

a. HAVE SUPPLIERS BILL YOU ON YOUR BEST DAY

There are probably only a couple of days each month when much of your revenue is physically received. Depending on your business and your location often this is on, or immediately following, major local paydays.

Instruct your regular suppliers to invoice you on those days. This will mean that you're paying your bills after you have received large amounts of cash from your customers or clients.

A few suppliers may balk at your request, saying it is impossible to change existing billing routine. Stick with it. After all, you're the customer in this case, and there's no reason why a simple request like this can't be accommodated.

How to do it: To save everyone's time, have a form letter written and printed on your company letterhead. State clearly the monthly billing day you prefer, and send it out to all your suppliers. Most won't even bother to argue the point; they'll make the change as you requested.

b. USE DISCOUNT DAY PAYMENT

To make their jobs easier, many bookkeepers prefer to pay bills just once or twice a month. As invoices come in they are set aside into one or two groups for the next payment date.

But that means most often that at least some bills are paid in advance of the final discount date. For example, an incoming bill is received on the 12th, with a discount date of the 22nd. But because your bookkeeper likes to pay bills just twice a month, on the 15th and 30th, the bill goes into the 15th group. When it is paid on the 15th it means that you have lost the use of that cash for seven days — until the 22nd when it was actually due — simply because your bookkeeper likes that simple system.

What to do: Instruct your bookkeeper to pay bills only on the date they are actually due. If this means paying one or two bills every day, the cost of her extra time is still more than offset by the free use of those funds.

And make sure that all discounts are taken. Not doing so is costly. For instance, if an invoice is marked "2% — 10 days, net 30 days," and you do not take the discount, you are in effect paying interest at the annual rate of 36%-plus for those extra 20% days. Even finance company funds would be a lot cheaper than that.

c. REFINANCE FIXED OBLIGATIONS

You may have a mortgage on your office or warehouse building or an installment note on delivery or office equipment. Consider rewriting those obligations over a longer period.

This will immediately reduce your current payments and free some cash for other needs. Even if the interest rate on the longer term is higher than your present rate, don't automatically discard the idea. Remember that with inflation — and despite government assurances to the contrary we can expect it to be here for some time — dollars paid in the future will be "cheaper" than present dollars. It's quite possible that with a new interest rate higher by say 2% or 3%, coupled with a continuing inflation fator of 8% or 10%, or even more — your net savings will be significant — in addition to the easing of cash payments now.

What to do: Have your bookkeeper send a letter to each creditor who holds a long term obligation from you. Instruct them to specify the exact terms and conditions under which they would rewrite the obligation over a longer term. When their replies come in you can quickly inspect them to see which should be rewritten in terms of present interest rates and probable future inflation rates.

d. SPREAD OUT MAJOR PURCHASES

Some managers and executives have a thing about cash and credit: they like to use the former to avoid the latter. This is commendable but today it's unrealistic.

Many suppliers now offer reasonable extended payment terms at no interest cost. If you purchase a photocopying unit, for example, the supplier may offer you the option of paying the balance over three or even six months at the cash price. Paying cash in this situation is foolish. Take whatever extended terms your suppliers will offer. Even if an interest cost is quoted, negotiate. On major purchases this item will often be waived. Or sometimes it makes sense to pay interest charged by suppliers. If a supplier charges an effective annual rate of 12 or 15%, while other sources of funds use an 18 or 24% rate, you may actually save money by stretching out payments on the purchase and at the same time paying off some other higher interest cost indebtedness.

How to do it: On all major purchases ask your supplier if the cash price can be paid over several months. More often than not he'll acquiesce, and you'll have interest-free use of those funds for a couple of months.

e. MAKE EVERY DAY A BILLING DAY

As with paying bills only once or twice a month, some bookkeepers prefer to issue bills or statements to customers just a few times each month because it's "easier." That it is. It's also costly for you.

There's no reason why bills and statements cannot be sent out every day. This is also sounder psychologically, because customers tend to pay bills faster when the reason for the bill is still fresh in their minds. Wait until the end of the month and they forget how important the product or service they bought was to them.

How to do it: Have your bookkeeper keep the last hour of each working day solely for sending out statements and bills. Even if there are only two or three bills to go, don't put them off until there's enough to make it worthwhile.

f. PLUG THE LOOPHOLES

Sometimes customers will use confusion as a reason for not promptly paying their accounts. For example, your bookkeeper might show a credit adjustment for a payment received from some third party, such as an insurance company. Yet with the typical shorthand notations used by bookkeepers, and often by computers, the reason for the credit adjustment may not be clear. Result: the customer holds off paying the bill until getting an explanation in person from your bookkeeper, or additional data from your computer.

When statements are sent out, they should be perfectly clear. Every dollar amount, whether debit or credit, should be fully explained. If there are charges for professional fees, they should be itemized in sufficient detail so that customers are clear as to what they're being charged for. Payments on account, and from whom, should be explained, along with any miscellaneous charges such as payments by you to a third party on the customer's behalf.

In short, the statement or bill should stand on its own feet with no further clarification needed. This will mean faster payments by customers and clients.

What to do: Tell your bookkeeper to keep accounting shorthand off statements. Make sure that bills and statements are clearly understandable to all customers. If you use a computer for statement preparation, make sure it is programmed to deliver understandable documents, not accounting gibberish.

g. KEEP AWARE OF PAST DUE ACCOUNTS

Some managers have no system for following up past due accounts. They wait until they're a year or so old, then either turn them over to a collection agency (generally with poor results at that late date) or they simply write them off as bad debts. Neither approach is sensible.

Have your bookkeeper flag or physically segregate accounts by 30-day periods. At the end of the first 30 days send out a friendly but firm form letter. Do the same at the end of 60 and 90 days, with each letter getting increasingly firm. Don't be embarrassed about this: tell your customers the truth, that you also have bills to pay, and that you expect them to pay theirs.

Most people are honest and well-intentioned, but if you treat their past due accounts as unimportant, you can hardly expect them to do otherwise.

How to do it: Instruct your bookkeeper to set up and use a 30, 60 and 90-day follow-up system for all accounts. In practice, form letters have proven just as effective as more costly and time-consuming personal letters, so use printed letters for each time period.

h. CUT OFF THE DEADBEATS

Unfortunately there will always be a few people who make a career of ignoring their debts. You have to decide at just what point you will draw the line, but there should be a line somewhere. When a customer reaches that point, send out a short letter explaining why you can no longer treat him on a credit basis. All future services will have to be on a cash basis.

Don't try to draw the matter out; as with all separations, a clean break is preferable to all concerned.

What to do: When a customer passes the credit cut-off point — which you have established in advance — instruct your bookkeeper to turn the account over to you. You then have to decide whether the customer is a deadbeat or an honest debtor in hard times. Follow your own feelings in the latter case. If the former, send out your "cash only" letter and, if it's worth the effort, place the account with a collection agency. But take positive action; then forget about the matter.

Use these eight pointers regularly and you'll soon find that your firm's cash position is strengthened, all without an extra dollar of injected capital.

10

TAXES

Up to now, as an employee you've probably only worried about filing an income tax form once a year, grumbled about paying sales tax whenever you wandered across the border into Washington or California to buy a few things, and automatically paid your property taxes as part of your mortgage payments. Right?

You might as well get used to one thing right away. If you're going to own a business, you will be involved in a lot more taxes. Every firm is subject to a whole string of them at the federal, state, and local level.

I'm not telling you this to discourage you, but rather, so that you will know what to expect and how to deal with the problem. Remember, there are millions of people in this country who work for someone else and think that it's great that business should pay so much in taxes. Unfortunately, there are a lot more of them than there are business owners. So, you can see why things have worked out this way.

Yet you can still survive and even make money under these circumstances. You see, every business (including your competitor) is faced with these same taxes. It's a necessary cost of doing business, just like paying the rent or utility bills. So, all you have to do is raise your prices accordingly. The trick is to look at the total tax structure, to see what you can do to claim an exemption here or a lower rate there. What you want to do is cut your total tax bill below your competition. We'll go into that a little later. Right now, I just want to show you what to expect.

a. FEDERAL TAXES

1. Department of Internal Revenue requirements
Newly-established businesses should apply for the "Mr. Businessman's Kit," available from any local IRS office. This kit contains the current employer's tax guide and all forms necessary to satisfy federal withholding requirements, such as application form SS-4 for the employer identification number, form W-4 for the employee's withholding certificate, the employer's quarterly federal tax return (for withheld income and social security taxes), form W-2 wage and tax statement for the current year, plus other forms which may be applicable to the particular type of business. Some of these are excise tax returns and federal use tax returns for highway motor vehicles or civil aircraft. The IRS maintains offices in Eugene, Medford, Portland, and Salem. The Portland office has a toll free number: 800-452-1980.

A particularly helpful publication prepared by the IRS, called "Tax Guide for Small Business," is published annually in plain layperson's language, and answers questions relating to corporations, partnerships, and sole proprietorships. It has 160 pages and is 75¢ per copy. It is available from most post offices or by writing to:

Superintendent of Documents
U.S. Government Printing Office
Division of Public Documents
Washington, D.C. 20402

Remittance is to be made by check or money order. Also, please refer to chapter 11 on "Organizing to Pay the Lowest Taxes Possible" for further tax information.

2. Social security administration requirements
Nearly all employees, employers, and self-employed people are required to participate in the social security program. For most occupations, social security contributions start with the first dollar earned. The major exceptions are agricultural employees and employers, who do not have to make contributions for those earning less than $150 (and meeting some other requirements).

Employers are required to withhold the appropriate percentage from an employee's pay and provide the employee with a receipt for this deduction. The employer has to keep records of each employee, match the employee's contribution, and make periodic deposits, usually with the quarterly income tax report, to the Internal Revenue Service. The employer also needs to record the employee's name and social security number exactly as it appears on his or her social security card.

Employees are required to have a social security card and contribute their share to the program by paycheck deductions. The contribution rates for the period starting January, 1977 are:

Employee pays: 5.85% of first $16,500 earned

Employer pays: 5.85% of first $16,500 paid to each employee

Self-employed pay: 8% of first $16,500 earned

Check List

Some of the Federal taxes for which a sole proprietor, a partnership, or a corporation may be liable are listed below.

If you:	You may be liable for:	You should use form:
Do business as a:		
(1) Corporation, association, etc.	Income tax	1120
(2) Corporation electing not to be taxed	Information return	1120S
(3) Partnership	Information return	1065
(4) Sole proprietor (or partner)	Income tax	1040
	Estimated tax	1040ES
	Self-employment tax	1040
Employ:		
1 or more persons	Income tax withholding	941
	FICA taxes	941
	FUTA tax	940
Furnish facilities for:		
Local and toll telephone service and teletypewriter exchange service	Excise tax on facilities	720
Transportation of persons or property by air		
Import:		
Adulterated or process butter	Stamp tax	923
Filled cheese		
Firearms	Occupational tax	11
Issue:		
Insurance policies (if you are a foreign insurer)	Excise tax	720
Maintain for use:		
Slot machines	Occupational tax	11-B
Punchboards	Occupational tax	11-C
	Wagering tax	730

Manufacture:

Adulterated or process butter	Occupational tax	11
	Stamp tax	218
Certain heavy duty trucks, buses, or trailers	Manufacturers excise tax	720
Beer	Excise tax	2034
Cigars, cigarettes, cigarette papers or tubes	Excise tax	2137, 2617, 3071
Distilled spirits	Excise tax	2521, 2522, 4077
Filled cheese	Occupational tax	11
	Stamp tax	218
Firearms	Occupational tax	11
	Manufacturers excise tax	720
	Stamp tax	1A (Firearms)
Fishing equipment	Manufacturers excise tax	720
Nonbeverage products subject to drawbacks	Occupational tax	11
Parts and accessories for trucks or buses	Manufacturers excise tax	720
Petroleum products		
Rectified spirits or wines	Occupational tax	11
	Excise tax	2523, 2527
Stills or condensers for use in distilling spirits	Occupational tax	11
	Commodity tax	11
Sugar	Manufacturers excise tax	720
Tires and tubes		
White phosphorus matches	Stamp tax	720
Wine	Excise tax	2050, 2052

Operate a:

Brewery	Occupational tax	11
Civil aircraft	Federal use tax	4638
Truck, truck-tractor, or bus on a highway	Federal use tax	2290
Wagering pool, lottery, or otherwise accept wagers	Occupational tax	11–C
	Wagering tax	730
Wholesale liquor dealership	Occupational tax	11

Sell at retail:

Adulterated butter	Occupational tax	11
Diesel and special fuels (including aviation fuels)	Retailers excise tax	720
Distilled spirits, wines, or beer	Occupational tax	11
Filled cheese		

Sell firearms:

Retail and wholesale under National Firearms Act of 1968	Occupational tax	11

Transfer:

Firearms	Stamp tax	4 (Firearms)

b. OREGON STATE TAXES

1. Income tax

Sole proprietors operating Oregon businesses pay their Oregon income tax by filing an Oregon individual income tax return. Partnerships must file a partnership return of income. This is merely a report, as the actual payment of tax is made by each partner on the individual income tax return. Personal income tax is based on federal taxable income with certain adjustments at the following rates:

First $500 of taxable income: 4%
Second $500: 5%
Next $1,000: 6%
Next $1,000: 7%
Next $1,000: 8%
Next $1,000: 9%
Over $5,000: 10%

Corporations file a corporation excise tax return and pay taxes directly. Rates for 1977 are 7% of net income *before paying federal income*. Rates are already scheduled to go to 7.5% of net income in 1978. Certain taxpayers are allowed to elect an alternative tax of either 1/4% or 1/8% on gross sales.

2. Unemployment insurance

As I mentioned earlier, unemployment insurance is required for any business having employees. You can debate whether to call this a tax or insurance. It is an insurance to the extent that premiums do pay for unemployment compensation and are based on experience. However, it is a tax in that it is mandatory. I'm sorry to say that the rates are among the highest in the country. The recent high unemployment has taken its toll. Currently the rate is 3% of the first $8,000 paid each employee.

3. Workers' compensation

Workers' compensation is another insurance almost like a tax. Rates vary by type of industry and are based on claim experience. However, regardless of which risk class you fall under, the cost is becoming substantial as medical costs keep rising.

Think what this means, though, if you are competing on your own, with a company having a lot of employees. They will be paying $240 a year for unemployment insurance for each employee, plus that much or even higher, for workers' compensation insurance. That's another good argument for operating a one-person business.

c. LOCAL TAXES

1. Property taxes

The primary support for cities, counties, and schools throughout the state is the property tax. Since different areas have different needs, the rates vary from city to city. For many businesses with minimal property investment, this variation will not be of much interest. However, if you have a large building and inventory, you will want to investigate which areas have the lowest rates. Actually, the inventory portion has become fairly insignificant, as it is being phased out. During 1977 inventory will only be taxed at 30% of the normal property tax rate. Each year the amount is reduced another 10%.

COMPARISON OF AVERAGE TAX RATES BY CITY
Dollars assessed per $1,000 of valuation

City	75-76	74-75	73-74
Albany	$29.65	$29.87	$28.42
Ashland	23.08	22.62	22.12
Astoria	28.22	29.71	30.45
Baker	25.22	25.33	25.77
Beaverton	30.29	33.32	—
Bend	25.64	27.31	24.42
Coos Bay	32.52	28.92	30.46
Corvallis	32.03	31.26	30.14
Dallas	29.33	28.97	25.44
Eugene	—	—	32.02
Forest Grove	25.05	25.11	—
Grants Pass	20.51	18.55	17.79
Gresham	30.18	29.61	27.82
Hillsboro	26.68	25.10	—
Klamath Falls	24.54	25.36	25.90
La Grande	—	29.68	24.49
Lake Oswego	—	27.02	28.78
Lebanon	33.09	32.10	27.75
McMinnville	30.28	24.57	29.90
Medford	—	23.55	—
Milwaukie	—	28.69	25.68
North Bend	31.63	34.92	31.13
Ontario	24.99	24.45	23.68
Oregon City	—	33.30	27.87
Pendleton	28.94	32.34	33.77
Portland	28.65	27.79	27.73
Roseburg	24.07	25.73	22.88
St. Helens	22.50	24.86	23.23
Salem	31.31	30.63	30.90
Salem	31.31	30.63	30.90
Salem	31.33	30.68	30.86
Springfield	—	—	29.19
The Dallas	28.55	27.32	28.28

Source: *Commerce Clearing House Reports.*

11
ORGANIZING TO PAY THE LOWEST TAXES POSSIBLE

It is a sad fact that the government has forced every astute business owner to become knowledgeable in tax laws if the business is to survive. Often the difference between success and failure is determined not by the technical proficiency of the owner, nor the ability to satisfy customers' needs, nor any of the other factors that you would generally consider important to run a successful business. Instead, the profit at the end of the year is determined by the ability of the owner or an accountant to take full advantage of all tax laws.

In this chapter, we'll explore the current laws to see how we can save tax dollars. Because it comes off the bottom line, every dollar saved from the tax collector is usually worth at least four dollars in extra sales.

Back in chapter 6, I discussed the three forms a business can take — proprietorship, partnership, and corporation. Just as each form offers a different degree of liability, each also provides different tax advantages.

a. SOLE PROPRIETORSHIPS

Proprietorships are always subject to at least two federal taxes — income and self-employment. All profit from this type of business is considered current income to the owner. This involves filling out Schedule C of 1040. The net profit (or loss) of the business is then reported as "Income other than Wages, Dividends, and Interest" on the owner's personal income tax report.

All profit of the business is taxed, whether or not it is withdrawn from the business. It can never be considered as a salary, and is, therefore, not deductible as an expense to the business. This may give you the impression that the proprietor has little flexibility in tax matters. Not true! You make a basic decision on whether to report income items on a cash basis, accrual basis, installment method, percentage of completion, or completed contract method.

Under the cash basis, we must report income in the taxable year received, and deduct all expenses in the taxable year paid. The Internal Revenue Service does require that you report under this method any amounts credited to your account and subject to your control. Electing the cash basis has this advantage over other methods. You may control income to the business during a high income year by postponing receipt of income until the next fiscal year. Conversely, you may increase deductions by prepaying interest (within certain limits) and taxes due later on. You can also get caught up on all outstanding bills at the end of the taxable year. On the other hand, you can postpone payment of bills to another year when the deductions may provide greater tax savings.

By using the "accrual basis," you report income that has been earned whether it is received or not. You deduct expenses that have been incurred, whether paid or not. This method has one advantage over the cash basis — it usually provides a more even and balanced income.

The other methods may be used if they clearly reflect your income. Hence, dealers in personal property may use the installment method, and construction contractors may use percentage of completion or completed contract methods. Descriptions of these methods may be found in IRS regulations.

b. PARTNERSHIPS

Partnerships offer interesting possibilities for reducing income taxes. Basically, all profit earned by the partnership is considered the personal income of the partners. Each partner must declare and pay taxes on whatever proportion is specified by the articles of co-partnership. Whether or not the profits are actually withdrawn from the business makes no difference in reporting. Salary to any partner, even if specified in the partnership agreement, is considered profit rather than wages. Although the partnership itself pays no income tax, a Form 1065 must be filed, reporting the income and its distribution.

One advantage in a partnership is that capital gains and certain other forms of income may be divided in different ways from normal income. If your partners are in a higher tax bracket, you can let them have a higher percentage of capital gains and less straight income. Some of your partners may find it to their advantage to receive all of the partnership's tax-exempt income or the dividend income. They can do this as long as they accept the economic risk of the presence or absence of such income.

A partnership has the same choice of accounting methods as the sole proprietorship — cash, accrual, etc. Complications can occur, though. For instance, if a partnership uses the accrual method, an individual partner with other businesses could be on a cash basis. In this case, the partner must count income reported by the partnership, whether it is received or not.

Depreciation offers another area to be examined by the partnership. Again, if you have partners with substantial incomes from other sources, they may prefer accelerated depreciation methods that give higher write-offs in the early years of the business. In other words, they may want their share of the partnership income to stay as low as possible. Yet, you probably need that income to be as high as possible in those early years. In this case, you want a straight line depreciation that will help level out income over the years. Give this careful consideration! Once you select a method, it's not easily changed.

How much is your inventory worth? The answer to that question can have a significant impact on your profits, whether it's a proprietorship, partnership, or corporation. Inventories can be valued at cost or the lower of cost or market value. However, should these values be applied on a "first-in first-out" (FIFO) basis, or on a "last-in first-out" (LIFO) basis? With the long term inflationary spiral we've had for the past generation, LIFO has become the preferred method. By using this method, inventory remaining at the end of a fiscal year is assumed to be composed of the earliest items received. During inflation, this will normally yield a lower value. You deduct this lower value for remaining inventory from the total cost paid for merchandise available for sale during the year. This will give a higher value for cost of merchandise sold. Taxable profits are reduced accordingly.

Still another aspect of partnerships is the possibility of making family members partners. By doing this, you can shift income from a family member in a higher tax bracket to one in a lower tax bracket. Looking at the family as a unit, the overall tax bill is reduced.

You can set up a family partnership, if capital is a major factor in producing income for the business. With a service-oriented partnership, a gift of an interest in the business will not be allowed, unless the new partner actually works in the business. Otherwise, gifts are allowed, but subject to examination by the Internal Revenue Service. If you are examined, just be prepared to show:

(a) That you made the gift while mentally competent
(b) That the person receiving the gift is competent
(c) That the gift was accepted
(d) That you actually transferred an equivalent share of control in the business.

c. CORPORATIONS

In contrast to the proprietorship or partnership, the earnings of a corporation are taxed directly. The corporate income tax rate is very simple — 22% of the first $25,000 earnings, and 48% of all earnings above that.

All salaries of employees and officers are considered legitimate expenses of the corporation, even if they are stockholders. Of course, these salaries are then taxed as personal income. Also, any dividends distributed by the corporation become personal income. In other words, if you establish a corporation, you will be dealing with a problem in double taxation.

If yours is a closely held corporation, you can take advantage of this. By controlling distribution of income between the corporation and yourself, you can achieve the minimum tax liability. Assuming that most of your shareholders are in higher tax brackets because of other sources of income, they will gain by keeping income in the corporation. Incidentally, in this case, a higher tax bracket would apply to anyone paying over 48%, which is what the corporation would be paying.

1. Should you be a Sub-chapter S corporation?

More than likely, you'll be in the other boat, where you need to shift as much income as possible to your personal use. This can be done in two ways:

(a) By paying yourself a higher salary, or

(b) By electing to be a Subchapter S corporation.

I can hear you asking: "What is a Subchapter S corporation?" Some years ago, Congress decided to assist small businesses. The result was incorporated into a Subchapter S added to the Internal Revenue Code. In effect, it gives you the opportunity to have the best of two worlds, lower tax rates and limited personal liability. It allows your corporation to elect to be taxed as a proprietorship or partnership.

However, there are a few restrictions:

(a) The corporation must have no more than 10 stockholders.

(b) There can be only one class of stock.

(c) All stockholders must be individuals or estates.

(d) The business must be a domestic corporation. (There is no problem here, since you'll be an Oregon corporation.)

(e) The company may not be a member of a group eligible to file consolidated returns.

(f) Over 80% of gross receipts must come from income other than royalties, rents, dividends, interest, annuities, gains on sales, exchanges of stock, or securities.

While there are technicalities to be observed, this election offers considerable advantages to small corporations. For instance:
- (a) Election as a Subchapter S corporation may be initiated or terminated as desired. So, you can use it in a year when it is advantageous, and not in a year when it is not an advantage.
- (b) In a high profit year, if you are a parent, you may give stock to your children to split your income, without giving up control of the corporation.
- (c) By establishing a different fiscal year for your corporation from your personal income tax year, you have the ability to shift income from a higher income year to a lower income year.
- (d) Stockholders can use corporate losses to shelter personal income from other sources.
- (e) Subchapter S income is not considered self-employment income, so it will not reduce or cancel social security benefits for retired members of a family-owned business.
- (f) The corporation is protected from a penalty tax on accumulated earnings.

How do you become a Subchapter S corporation? It's fairly simple. You and your fellow shareholders may elect to do so anytime during the month preceding or in the first month of the taxable year. A form 2553 must be filed with all shareholders signing a consent.

There are some drawbacks to this election that you should be aware of. Probably, the most important one is that buying and selling stock becomes very complex. The law requires that annual gains or losses be distributed to stockholders in proportion to their length of ownership. As you can imagine, mid-year transactions become very complicated.

2. The Domestic International Sales Corporation

Now, we come to another form of corporation of particular value to many Oregon firms — the Domestic International Sales Corporation (better known as the DISC). Under this form, any company involved in export sales gains a very attractive tax advantage. To stimulate more exports, and thereby regain a favorable balance of trade, Congress granted eligible firms electing to be DISCs a 50% deferment on income taxes. The other half is taxed directly to the shareholders, only when distributed, when a shareholder sells out, or when the corporation no longer qualifies under the program.

Income that is taxed to shareholders is treated as dividends. However, these dividends are not eligible for the 85% or 100% deductions on intercorporate dividends.

The DISC must have at least 95% of its income derived from export sales or rentals. Most firms involved in international sales accomplish this by setting up a subsidiary corporation just to handle the export sales of the business. Typically, the parent corporation sells products to the DISC at cost, so that all profits from export sales accrue to the DISC.

As usual, there are a few other qualifications. At least 95% of the assets must be export assets. Only one class of stock is allowed. Finally, at least $2,500 in capital must be retained throughout the taxable year. You can see that these are details which can be handled with a little care. Election as a DISC is made on Form 4876 and must be consented to by each shareholder.

12
OPERATING TO PAY THE LOWEST TAXES POSSIBLE

So far we've talked about how to locate and organize your business in order to pay the lowest taxes. The job doesn't stop there. Wherever you locate or however you organize, there are many things you can do while operating your business to gain full advantage of existing tax laws. Let's look at some of these.

a. HOW TO LOWER YOUR TAXABLE INCOME

There are many ways to reduce your taxable income legally, and you should take advantage of every legitimate expense. As a self-employed business person, you are entitled to deduct all expenses incurred for the purpose of earning income. To take advantage of these expenses, such as car expenses, meals, and entertainment, it is absolutely necessary for you to keep detailed receipts.

I know that many people think it's a pain in the neck to get receipts and keep them. Many have "friends" who have told them what they can claim without being questioned. Well, *they are wrong!* They are so wrong, that when you — the poor taxpayer — who has acted in good faith, are audited, the whole claim (or a major portion of it) will be thrown out the window.

If you are entitled to claim expenses, it is not too much trouble to keep receipts. Every time you keep the receipt for $2 from the Dairy Queen or the A & W, you have just put another *tax-free dollar* in your pocket. You must keep receipts. These receipts *must* be itemized and totalled.

There are only two places where you cannot get a receipt for tax purposes — parking meters and pay telephones. In both cases, you should keep a diary of these expenses. They do mount up. One fellow I know kept notes of what he spent in a year for these items after years of thinking them unimportant. He guessed $50 for the year. He kept a record for the next nine months, and in nine months had spent $435, almost as much per month as he had guessed for a year. This meant an extra refund of over *$250 tax-free.* Remember, that will be every year for many years to come.

As sure as death itself, sooner or later, you will encounter problems with the tax department if you do not keep receipts, especially when you are running your own business.

Now, we shall take a brief look at the more important ways of reducing taxes.

b. USING YOUR HOME FOR YOUR BUSINESS

Earlier, we discussed the advantages of not having employees in your business. One big extra to this is the possibility of operating your business in your home. As we saw in chapter 5, you not only save the cost of buying or renting another location, you also gain a deduction for maintenance and depreciation expenses of those areas being used for your business.

You will be required to establish that you regularly use a specific part of the home for your business. Once established, you can deduct the portion of items such as rent, electricity, taxes, and interest on a mortgage assignable to that part of the home. Full deductions are allowable for painting and repairs in the work area. Portions of roof repairs and exterior painting are also allowed. A portion of the overall depreciation calculated on a straight-line basis is also allowed.

Caution: Recent changes in regulations make it absolutely necessary that whatever portions of your home are used for business must be solely devoted to that to be allowed. So, arrange your working and living areas carefully!

More details on operating a business in your home are available in IRS publication 587. This is sold by:

The Superintendent of Documents
U.S. Government Printing Office
Washington, D.C. 20402
Price: 30¢.

c. USING YOUR AUTOMOBILE IN THE BUSINESS

Just as you can pro-rate part of your home expenses to your business, you can also claim a portion of your car expenses as business expenses.

The main thing to remember about car expenses is that the IRS requires more detailed information than most taxpayers are inclined to give. To claim car expenses, *all* expenses must be recorded and kept. It is not enough to only write down or keep expenses for when you were actually working — such as the gas expense when you went to see a supplier in Portland. You must keep all the year's expenses. In that way, major repairs, tires, insurance, and the capital cost allowance are spread over both personal and business portions.

It has been my experience that small businesspeople penalize themselves when they do not keep proper car records. If you really hate to keep a lot of details on your car, you can reduce paperwork considerably by taking a standard allowance. In recent years, this has been 12¢ per mile for the first 15,000 miles of business use and 9¢ per mile over that.

On the other hand, if you really want to get the maximum deduction, here's what you can include:
  (a) Gas and oil (including state and local taxes)
  (b) Repairs
  (c) Parking charges, bridge tolls, ferry tolls
  (d) Towing charges
  (e) Washing, waxing, and polishing
  (f) Lubrication and greasing
  (g) Garage expenses
  (h) Antifreeze and other supplies
  (i) Tires, tubes, and accessories lasting less than one year
  (j) Depreciation
  (k) License fees (including driver's license)
  (l) Interest on loan to buy the car

(m) Insurance

(n) State and local taxes

(o) Motor club membership

All these may be allocated to your business on the basis of the percentage of miles travelled on business to the total number of miles travelled.

d. BUSINESS ENTERTAINMENT

Many businesses, particularly those where individual sales become fairly large, find it necessary to entertain customers. Although this is an actual legitimate expense to the business, you must be very careful to document it properly. Treasury regulations require two types of records:

(a) A diary, account book, or other record, listing the background and details, and

(b) Receipts

Altogether, these records must show:

(a) The amount of each entertainment cost

(b) The date of entertainment

(c) Whether it was in conjunction with business discussion

(d) Details of that discussion

(e) Name, address, and description of type of entertainment

(e) Business reason or business benefit derived

(f) Who was entertained

e. MAINTENANCE AND REPAIRS

What is maintenance? What are repairs? When do repairs turn into an addition?

Maintenance is the general upkeep of an asset. It refers to routine painting, oiling, replacing filters, rubber hoses, etc. Repairs refers to a breakdown. If it won't work or is unsuitable because of mechanical condition, it should be considered a repair. The problem starts when the "repair" becomes materially better than the original was or ever could be.

If a store roof is leaking and the owner patches it with some asphalt, it is a repair. If the roof leaks and the owner prices out the repair and decides that for a bit or even a lot more, he/she can raise the roof and put in another mezzanine floor, then it is an addition, even though it was prompted by the need for a repair.

The difference is that a repair may be listed as an expense line in the current year. An addition must be added to the capital cost of the asset, and depreciated over a number of years. Also, if the addition is depreciated and then sold for more than the depreciated value, there would be a "recapture" of depreciation, and tax would have to be paid on the recapture. It is easy to see that it is to the advantage of the taxpayer to try and "expense" the item. The IRS will always check into large "repair" items.

f. OFFICE EXPENSES, POSTAGE, AND STATIONERY

I am just as guilty here as anyone. It seems that I always pay for an office expense out of my pocket, and then forget to collect the money from petty cash. Every time you spend $2 for postage and don't record the expenditure, you have just thrown $1 in tax saving out the window. I suggest that if you make it a habit to always take the money from petty cash to buy a small item, your balancing of the petty cash will force you to remember the receipt. Petty cash should be balanced nightly for this reason.

g. MEDICAL AND DENTAL EXPENSES

Once your business has its head above water, you should look into instituting medical, dental, and possibly group term life insurance plans for yourself and your employees. Unfortunately, you can't institute policies just for yourself (and your family) where the business pays the premiums and claims an expense. It must be open for all full-time employees for the expense to be deductible. The deduction can be the entire premium, as long as it does not discriminate against some employees.

Even with these restrictions, if you operate a very small business (two to three persons) the expense is justified because, if you want, you can have the employees (including yourself) pay half, the company the other half, and you have complete health protection at a very reasonable rate. Besides, it is a nice fringe benefit for the employees.

h. TAX PAYMENTS

I have only one observation to make here. If you find yourself in that uncomfortable position of not having enough funds to make a tax payment on time, don't panic. Most of all, don't run out and pay some exorbitant interest on a loan to pay it with. Always try to file your tax returns on time, but remember that almost all tax laws make allowance for late payment. Most of these were written in a day and age when interest rates were much lower than they are today. So, many times you will be far better off to pay the penalties and interest to the government.

i. SELF-EMPLOYED RETIREMENT PLANS

In 1974, Congress passed a new law allowing self-employed people to set up individual retirement programs. You can now contribute up to 15% of your net earnings, not to exceed $7,500, to a qualified pension or profit-sharing plan for yourself. These contributions are deductible from your current income. Earnings on funds in the plan accumulate on a tax-free basis. No taxes are paid until benefits are drawn (normally at retirement).

13

WHAT ABOUT BUYING A BUSINESS?

a. WHY BUY A BUSINESS?

One short-cut to success is to buy a business. By buying instead of starting a business, you avoid many of the initial problems, and you already have a proven market and profit picture.

However, there always seems to be a price to pay; and in this case there are really two prices. One is money, and the second is time and effort. If you buy a prosperous business, the money you lay out for good will is paying for these advantages. This may be money well spent. On the other hand, it may be entirely wasted, if the business is really a failing one or has unforeseen problems. The lesson here, then, is: before you invest — investigate.

This brings us to the second price of buying a business, and that is time and effort. Buying a business is a little like buying a house. You should look at many, many prospects before making an offer. By doing this, your perception of what you are really looking for is increased immeasurably. So, if you can afford this kind of time — not many of us can — you are probably further ahead to buy a business.

Every day several dozen Oregon businesses change hands. For buyers and sellers alike, such changes of ownership are major events. The process is complex. A clear understanding of it, and careful planning of each step are needed for a logical, unemotional, and right decision. The transaction can then be closed in the proper legal form, safe and fair for both parties.

This chapter outlines some of the key considerations involved in both buying and selling a business. For simple illustration, the case of a proprietorship is used, although similar considerations will apply to partnerships and to companies. In any case, it is essential that both the buyer and seller invest enough effort in preliminary work in order to avoid a waste of everyone's time and money.

b. LOCATING AND PURCHASING A BUSINESS

1. Careful selection

Select the size and type of business best suited to your interests, character, capital available, and prior experience. The selection of the type of business is a personal one, and we discussed the important considerations to keep in mind in chapter 3.

2. Seeking opportunities

Seek out opportunities which meet your requirements. This may be done by:
- (a) Word-of-mouth contact which, by itself, is probably the least effective means, unless you know of an interested party willing to negotiate
- (b) Classified newspaper advertising which is effective, provided that the advertisement is specific as to price, location, and size of the business
- (c) Real estate brokers who specialize in business opportunities and who can help you in finding and screening businesses *and* in ensuring that all the proper legal steps are taken
- (d) Trade publications which are effective in advertising businesses specializing in that particular trade. (If you are looking for a particular kind of business, this method eliminates a lot of time.)

3. Properly evaluate each opportunity

The evaluation of each opportunity on a comparative basis is the most crucial stage. Make sure you have satisfactory answers on all the following:
- (a) The reason the business is up for sale
- (b) Its assets and liabilities
- (c) Its history, location, and potential
- (d) Its profit record, operating ratios, and projections

Do not rush your investigations; time taken to get the necessary information will pay off in deciding whether to purchase and at what price. Many successful business owners report that they considered alternatives for a year or more before deciding to go ahead.

An adverse trend apparent from the financial statements may reveal the true reason for selling; and you should establish the reasons for such a trend, and determine whether it is reversible or whether, for example, changes in the character of the neighborhood are responsible.

One of the principal assets often involved in a change of ownership is the inventory. A physical count (preferably by an independent appraiser) should be taken to establish a fair price for it, having regard to whether it is saleable, to its condition and style, and after making due allowance for any items that would have to be cleared out at a loss.

Similarly, the accounts receivable should be analyzed for quality and aging. This simple analysis is an indication of the seller's credit and collection policies and of the level of operating capital required to support day-to-day operations.

If real estate is involved, a professional appraisal of its value might be money well-spent, since its condition and versatility should be reflected in the price offered. What alterations are needed and at what cost? Similarly, the furniture, fixtures, and equipment should be assessed.

Also, be sure to determine that there are no hidden liabilities, such as unregistered liens against equipment, back taxes, or pending lawsuits. An accountant's or lawyer's help at this stage would be wise. The agreement of purchase and sale should spell out that all claims not shown on the balance sheet used as the basis of sale are the responsibility of the seller.

4. Establishing a fair price

Establishing a fair price is the biggest problem. The seller understandably tries to put a price on the effort and money invested in the business. However, you are mainly interested in the ability of the business to yield a good return on your investment, after allowing for a reasonable salary. In other words, you want to do more than just buy a job.

Therefore, the future potential is of primary interest to determine whether the business will yield a return on investment at least equal to, if not better than, alternative sources. If such is not the case, you shouldn't offer more than the value of the tangible assets. As the term suggests, these are assets which can be touched, weighed, or measured, and have real value. You would not ascribe any value to "good will", which in one sense, is directly related to the earning power and potential of the business. Good will can be best described as that amount in excess of what the business is worth.

You must convince the seller to forget about prior investment of money and effort, and base the price realistically on present and future factors. I suggest that the following steps in determining a price formula might be useful:

(a) Establish the tangible net worth of the business (that is, assets less liabilities, ignoring any intangible assets, such as good will).

(b) Estimate what dollar return (perhaps 10%) an outside investor would get on this amount if invested elsewhere with approximately the same degree of risk. This is called "earning power."

(c) Add a reasonable salary for yourself.

(d) Establish from the operating statements the average annual net earnings before taxes (net profit before deducting owner's drawings) for the past few years. This gives a means of comparing the historical earnings with those you could get from alternative sources open to you. The trend of historical earnings is the key factor.

(e) Deduct the earning power (b) plus reasonable salary (c) from the average net earnings (d) to determine the business's "extra earning power."

(f) To value the intangibles, multiply (e) by the number of years of profitable operation. A well-established and successful business would justify using a factor of five or more; a less well-based enterprise might be fairly priced at a factor of three.

(g) Final offering price equals tangible net worth (a) plus value of intangibles (f).

Example

Let's apply the price formula I have described to evaluate two businesses up for sale:

	Business A	Business B
(a) Tangible net worth	$40,000	$40,000
(b) Earning power — 10% of (a)	4,000	4,000
(c) Reasonable salary for owner	10,000	10,000
(d) Average net earnings	16,000	10,000
(e) Extra earning power (d) minus (b) and (c)	2,000	4,000
(f) Value of intangibles (e) times 5	10,000	Nil
Final offering price (a) plus (f)	$50,000	$40,000

In the case of business A, we see that the seller should get a substantial price of $10,000 for the intangibles (mainly "good will"), because the business is well-established, and is probably earning more than you would likely get elsewhere with comparable effort and risk. You would, in this example, recover the cost of good will (f) in five years. The reasoning is that if the business continues to average $16,000 net earnings per year, you will realize your 10% return of $4,000, a salary of $10,000, plus $2,000 in extra earnings each year. This last amount would equal, in five years, the $10,000 you paid initially for the good will.

For business B, there is no good will value, because there is no extra earning power (e), and you might even conclude that the business was not worth its tangible net worth (a), because of the poor return on an investment of that size. Intangible assets often include patents, franchises, organization expense, trade marks, and good will.

5. Ensure that the transaction is handled properly

Making sure the transaction is handled properly is very important. But, provided you have followed the preceding steps, you should not be far off the track.

First, when negotiations look as though they're getting serious, contact a lawyer and an accountant. Make sure both persons have experience in this area — because many do not. You need a lawyer to make sure that you are getting what you are paying for, and you need an accountant to arrange everything to your advantage with regard to paying taxes.

Again, if you don't know a good lawyer or accountant, ask your friends who are in business. They will be in the best position to know, and are almost always willing to help.

Caution: In case the business you intend to buy requires any type of license that involves more than the routine filling out of an application and paying a fee, be careful. Make sure that you do not close the sale until you have that license fully transferred to you. The business might be worthless to you without the license. Even a few weeks' delay in receiving a liquor license, for instance, can be disastrous to certain types of grocery stores.

c. FINANCING THE TRANSACTION

The financing of the transaction must now be considered, assuming that you and the seller have reached an agreement on the price. Remember not to put all your funds into the purchase price! You will need enough left over for operating capital and personal expenses, until the business can begin paying you a salary. Perhaps the seller will be willing to finance part of the sale. That is, he or she may make a loan to you, possibly secured by a mortgage on the business's fixed assets, and repayable with interest over a term acceptable to both of you. Remember that whether the transaction is on an all-cash basis or partly financed, this should not affect the selling price.

d. CONCLUSION

The main thing to remember in buying a business is to insist on full disclosure of all facets of the business you are interested in purchasing. Do not be stampeded into making a snap decision. Insist on adequate time to do the necessary research, which could also involve seeking the advice of an accountant, a lawyer, and possibly, a real estate agent.

14

WHAT ABOUT FRANCHISING?

a. INTRODUCTION

If you are starting a small retail or service business of your own, or even if you just want to expand your present business, you might consider franchising.

Franchising reduces your risks because the reputation of the franchised product or service helps to ensure sales, and because the management assistance and advice which many franchisors provide contribute to profits.

This "revolution" in busines has caught the imagination of many small businesspeople, and there are good reasons for it.

If you are a small investor, franchising can minimize your risk of failure by allowing you to start in business under the image of a corporate name and trademark, and by offering you training and management assistance from experienced personnel. Sometimes, you may also be offered financial assistance, so that you can get started in a business of your own with less than the usual amount of cash.

In addition, franchising makes it possible for you, the small investor, to be associated with a regional, national, and sometimes international organization. From the standpoint of companies offering franchises — the franchisors — this type of business operation makes possible rapid expansion.

Whether or not you are ready for franchising depends on several things, your present situation being one. Are you thinking of closing out your present business and opening a franchise business, or do you intend to start a franchise operation? Maybe you are considering the possibility of adding a franchised line, or lines, to an existing business. However, before you decide, think carefully about how much of your independence you would have to give up.

As in any other type of business undertaking, your return in franchising is related directly to the amount of time and money you invest. Contrary to what some people may think, franchising is not a get-rich-quick deal. Nor is it an easy road to expansion for the franchisor — the manufacturer or distributor. There are dangers in franchising, for both franchisor and franchisee.

However, you can largely avoid the pitfalls when you know what franchising is and understand its advantages and disadvantages. You should also know where and how to get the facts to evaluate the prospects and profit potential of a franchise opportunity.

b. WHAT IS FRANCHISING?

Franchising is essentially a system of distribution under which an individually-owned business is operated as though it were part of a large chain, complete with trade marks, uniform symbols, design, equipment, and standardized services or products. Franchising can be used for almost any type of business.

As a marketing technique, franchising is uniquely American. It began before the turn of the century, when automobile manufactrers and petroleum refiners licensed new car dealers and gasoline service stations to retail their products in assigned areas. These retailers were supported with nation-wide advertising and publicity. From these beginnings, the idea was picked up for quick-food-service places, rent-a-car businesses, drug stores, and auto parts stores. Soon added were such services as dance studios and janitorial services.

Franchising began to flourish after World War II because opportunities were offered to small investors to operate franchised roadside business (primarily drive-in food and ice cream stands). When such drive-ins began to spread all over the American landscape, franchising became a magic word.

Today, hundreds of companies market many products and services through franchised outlets. Moreover, some of the best-known and oldest names in American industry are using franchised stores to expand into new markets with new or established products and services.

c. THE FRANCHISE CONTRACT

The license, or franchise contract, is your key to franchising success. But it can also contain the seeds for disappointment and discontent, which can cause failure for both you, the investor, and the parent company.

In effect, a franchise contract is an investment agreement between the franchisor — sometimes known as the parent company — and the franchisee — the investor. Contracts may range from a simple one-page memorandum of agreement to highly complex documents, in which every conceivable detail of business operation is spelled out.

In some instances, contracts, in addition to specifying the exact products and services which a franchise may sell under the parent company's name, dictate the hours and days of business, as well as the types of uniforms (if any) to be worn by franchisees and their employees.

You should bear in mind that there is no standard franchise agreement any more than there is a uniform code of business practice, nor is there any special significance in a simple contract as compared with a complex one. A great deal depends on the type of business being franchised and the method the parent company uses for selecting franchisees.

In all cases, however, you should never sign a franchise contract without legal counsel. Today, the most reputable franchising companies insist that prospective investors do not sign until they have consulted attorneys or at least close family advisors, friends, accountants, or their bankers.

Although practically no two franchise contracts are alike, certain essential elements should be checked or questioned if they are not present in contracts.

(a) Is there a franchise fee? If so, what is the basis for it?
(b) Are there continuing royalties?

- (c) What is the total cash investment required, and what are the terms for financing the balance?
- (d) How do the cash investment and payments compare with other similar franchises?
- (e) Will you be required to participate in company-sponsored promotion and publicity, by contributing a percentage of profits to an "advertising fund?" If so, will you have the right to veto any increase in contributions to the "fund?'"
- (f) If the parent company's product or service is protected by patent or liability insurance, is the same protection extended to you?
- (g) Under what conditions may your franchise be cancelled?
- (h) What special form of continuing assistance does the parent company obligate itself to give you after you are operating the business?
- (i) Under what terms may you sell the business, to whomever you please, at whatever price you may be able to obtain?
- (j) Will you be compelled to sell any new products introduced by the parent company after you have opened the business?
- (k) How can you terminate your agreement if you are not happy for some reason?
- (l) Will you have an exclusive territory?
- (m) In essence, does the course you want to take parallel that of the franchisor? Does his/her success depend upon your success?

d. ADVANTAGES AND DISADVANTAGES

Generally, the principal advantage of franchising is that it enables you, as an investor, to capitalize on experience that you might otherwise have to obtain the hard way — through trial and eror. The parent company uses its experience in business locations, management, advertising, publicity, product research, and development, to enable its franchisees to start and operate its outlets with optimum efficiency, maximum profitability, and minimum friction.

When the company's products are proven and well-known products, your business has an "instant" pulling power. On your own, it would probably take years of promotion and considerable investment to build such an identity and good will.

Yet, by franchising, you will lose your personal identity to that of the parent company, which has tremendous sums of money invested in building and maintaining its identity for your use. So, if you enjoy having your business known by your name, a franchise business may not be for you. On the other hand, consider the increased sales and profits which you might make with a franchise arrangement. Consider all sides of the question. Then make your decision.

Remember, though, that in a franchise operation, you cannot make all the rules. Contrary to the many "be your own boss" lures in franchise advertisements, you may not truly be your own boss. The extent to which you are the captain of your own ship depends on the franchise contract.

You may have no effective voice in deciding your own future or the products you want to sell. And, as was mentioned earlier in this section, your hours and days of business may be specified in the contract. You have to live by the rules of your franchise contract. So, be sure that they are acceptable to you before you sign it.

Perhaps a brief look at the parent company's side will be helpful in understanding some of the rules that are in the contract. Manufacturers or distributors start franchising operations to trade proven experience and known product accpetance for your money and time. Thus, their sales can be increased at lower cost, than if they, alone, had to put up all the money.

A big problem for the franchisor is that of picking the right kind of people to run the franchised outlets. The parent company has the disadvantage of having to deal with individuals who, when they become successful, may forget about the parent company's "helping hand" that boosted them to prosperity. "They've got nothing to offer me," is the way some of these businesspeople feel at this stage, thinking that they could have been successful without the parent company.

Even when the right kind of people are chosen, the franchisor has serious problems in administration and control. After all, the franchisees are individual small businesspeople — not company-employed managers. Therefore, a reputable parent companies tries to use a contract containing rules with which both the company and the outlet operator can live in a team framework, if not in a team spirit.

e. HOW FRANCHISEES ARE CHOSEN

When you seek a franchise which you feel is right for you, you may be disappointed if you aren't aware of how manufacturers and distributors choose their franchisees. They get prospects in a variety of ways. Most advertise for them in the "business opportunities" sections of newspapers and magazines. Some rely entirely on the word-of-mouth recommendations of their existing franchisees, and others recruit franchisees through exhibits at trade shows and business conventions.

The final selection of franchisees depends on many things. Some parent companies, for instance, will not select any franchisee who does not agree to accept a minimum period of training. Others require psychological or aptitude tests. Still others rely entirely on comprehensive questionnaires and personal interviews.

Sometimes, the process begins with a parent-company's representative interviewing the prospective franchisee in his/her home. This interview is followed by a final interview at the parent company's headquarters. If you refuse to travel to headquarters for this interview, many franchisors will disqualify you immediately. They feel that such a refusal indicates a lack of real interest in the opportunity they offer.

f. FINDING THE RIGHT FRANCHISE

When looking for a franchise that is right for you, you should watch out for the "fast buck" operators, sometimes called "front money people." Essentially, they offer nothing more than the sale of equipment and a catchy business name. Once they sell you the equipment, they do not care whether you succeed or fail.

Be certain that you are dealing with a reputable company. One of the best techniques for checking is to ask the company to provide you with a list of its existing franchisees in the area which you are considering. From this list, you should select several names, and visit their offices during business hours.

By spending at least a few hours at each location, you can get an idea of what's going on. How many customers come in? What do they buy? What amount? And so on. You should also take time to ask the franchisees about the business. Most good parent companies encourage their franchisees to answer all questions by prospective investors.

When checking on a parent company, you should ask these important questions:

(a) When was the business established?
(b) Will its owners give me a specimen contract to study with the advice of legal counsel?
(c) How does the company provide continuing assistance for its franchisees? Are there supervisors who visit regularly, or only when called to help solve problems?
(d) How does the company resolve its differences with franchisees?
(e) How many franchisees are now operating?
(f) What has been the "mortality" or failure rate among franchisees, and what happens if I become broke?
(g) Am I locked into buying my supplies from the franchisor, and if so, how am I guaranteed that the franchisor's supplies and services will remain competitive?
(h) What advertising assistance does the franchisor offer?

g. WHAT DO YOU REQUIRE FROM A FRANCHISE?

To be a successful franchisee, you must choose a business on the basis of understanding your own needs and requirements. Some people either overlook, or are not aware of the fact, that franchising requires as much hard work as any other business. The parent company teaches you, but nobody will do the work for you.

To choose wisely in franchising, you should list your requirements for success by asking yourself the following questions:

(a) Why do I want a franchised business, rather than one I'd have to start entirely on my own?

(b) Am I capable of accepting supervision, even though I will presumably be my own boss?

(c) Am I prepared to accept rules and regulations with which I may not agree?

(d) Will I be content with owning only one business location, where I may not be able to expand as I desire?

(e) Can I afford the period of training involved?

(f) What are my strengths and weaknesses and how do they fit in with the strengths and weaknesses of the franchise company?

For example, if you have a promotional flair, a franchisor who offers advertising assistance may not be of much help to you. On the other hand, if keeping a place clean is a problem, regular inspections and cleanliness standards set by the franchisor would be a bonus.

If you have never been in business for yourself, you should ask yourself whether you have enough confidence to be a self-starter after training and close supervision is over. After all, the unknown quantity in franchising is the person who seeks a franchise. Have you made an honest evaluation of your desires, abilities, and willingness to work within a co-operative framework?

15
THE INS AND OUTS OF THE IMPORT/EXPORT BUSINESS

As I mentioned earlier, Oregon is strategically situated to handle a large volume of foreign trade. For this reason it is worth going into some detail on the actual mechanics of importing or exporting.

Many people shy away from this field because they think it involves complex paperwork, language barriers, and monetary difficulties far too complicated for a small business. To a degree this is true. However, 60% of all American firms engaged in exporting have fewer than 100 employees. So it can't be too bad. Sure, there are monetary difficulties, but there are well-established methods of handling funds in international trade. To make it even simpler, 90% of all world trade is transacted with American dollars. As for the language barrier, English is the principal language used in international commerce. So the need for translation comes up rarely. When it does, translation services are usually readily available. This leaves us with complex paperwork as the only real obstacle. Master this and you're in business. So let's look at what is really involved.

a. WHERE TO START
New import or export firms should plan on contacting three key service organizations when starting: the U.S. Department of Commerce, an international bank, and a foreign freight forwarder. The U.S. Department of Commerce is located at 501 Pittock Building, 921 S.W. Washington Street, Portland, Oregon 97205. If you go into the import/export business you can almost regard these three organizations as your partners. All successful companies utilize them to various degrees. There is some

overlap of services between them, but each has an area of expertise. For instance, the U.S. Department of Commerce can help you by doing the following:

(a) Pinpointing markets overseas
(b) Analyzing foreign markets
(c) Suppling sales leads
(d) Supplying market research reports on various products
(e) Providing details on foreign firms
(f) Organizing trade shows
(g) Directing you to appropriate organizations

An international bank can assist you in these ways:

(a) Assisting you to locate new markets
(b) Supplying data on the business climate in each country
(c) Introducing you to an overseas buyer
(d) Advising you on developments which might affect trade
(e) Investigating the credit of foreign firms
(f) Advising you on financial aspects of transactions
(g) Providing import/export financing
(h) Assisting with documents and transmittal of funds
(i) Arranging for insurance

These Oregon banks have international departments:

The Bank of California,
407 S.W. Broadway, Portland

The Bank of Tokyo, Ltd.
411 S.W. 6th, Portland

Canadian Imperial Bank of Commerce
504 S.W. 6th, Portland

First National Bank of Oregon
1300 S.W. 5th, Portland

The Oregon Bank
319 S.W. Washington, Portland

United States National Bank of Oregon
309 S.W. 6th, Portland

A foreign freight forwarder can assist you in the following ways:
- (a) Providing routing and scheduling data
- (b) Booking cargo space
- (c) Quoting rates and other costs
- (d) Advising you on license and consular requirements
- (e) Preparing shipping documents
- (f) Providing marking and labelling requirements
- (g) Assuring appropriate packing
- (h) Taking care of shipping insurance
- (i) Arranging for storage in a warehouse
- (j) Arranging for safe delivery to the buyer

Oregon freight forwarders include:

General Freight Services, Inc.,
Oregon Pioneer Building, Portland

Ted L. Rausch Company of Oregon
Oregon Pioneer Building, Portland

Seaport Shipping Company
4610 S.E. Belmont, Portland

J. T. Steeb & Co., Inc.
Oregon Pioneer Building, Portland

b. EXPORTING

Exporters have a basic choice in their method of distribution; it can be either direct or indirect. Indirect distribution is probably the best choice for a newcomer. This method involves no contact between you and the overseas buyer. Instead you rely on professional export management companies (EMC). A full service EMC can research foreign markets for you, appoint overseas distributors or representatives, handle all promotional and marketing activities, and take care of the delivery of your products. Another version of indirect distribution involves a cooperative "piggy back" approach. Here you pay a carrier, which would normally be a large manufacturer with established markets overseas, to handle your product along with its own. (One of the services of the Department of Commerce is to try to match riders with carriers.)

As you gain confidence in your own abilities to handle work overseas, you can move into direct exporting. This will normally involve appointing an overseas sales representative who will work much as a manufacturer's representative does in this country — on a commission basis. Another way involves establishing sales agreements with foreign distributors who will purchase direct from you and handle all marketing themselves.

Overseas promotion can be handled like promotion in this country. You should be careful, however, to consult with your distributors or others knowledgeable in the area you're dealing in to avoid conflicts with foreign cultures, goofs in translation of ad material, etc. A well-used device by many export firms is to promote their product at international trade shows. Hundreds are held every year around the world. (The U.S. Department of Commerce sponsors many of these.) Others are sponsored by state and local trade organizations. Usually a given trade show will specialize in certain products which have the most potential in the country where the show is being held.

Financing export sales brings the international bank into play. Transactions in foreign trade frequently require four to six months to complete. Needless to say, this can create a serious cash flow problem for even a well-financed firm. International banks can ease this by:

(a) providing working capital loans

(b) purchasing export receivables

(c) loaning on shipping and collection documents

(d) making direct loans to foreign importers

(e) providing floor plan loans to your overseas dealer

(f) advancing funds against a letter of credit

Credit checks become even more important in international trade than in domestic sales. The long distances involved, the problems of legal recourse, and difficulties in repossession make it imperative that you know that your buyer is reputable. Your international bank, the U.S. Department of Commerce, and other American firms dealing with foreign firms will be your main sources of credit information. Cash in advance or consignment sales are not normally used in international trade. The most common methods of payment are draft collections, letters of credit, and open account sales.

1. Draft collections

A draft is the basic document supporting the payment claim of a seller from a buyer. It is the seller's written order to the buyer to pay a given amount by a certain date. A draft payment arranged through international banks is called a draft collection. Here's how the process works: (1) The exporter and importer arrange a sale with an agreement that the payment will be by draft collection. (2) The exporter makes the shipment, fills out a draft form and collection instruction sheet, and turns them over to a bank, along with any documents requested by the importer. (3) That bank then sends the draft and documents to its overseas branch or a correspondent bank near the importer. (4) That second bank contacts the importer when the draft and documents have arrived. (5) The importer pays the second bank and picks up the documents. (6) Those documents allow the importer to pick up the shipment from the carrier. (7) The second bank transmits the importer's payment to the first bank. (8) Finally the first bank turns the payment over to the exporter.

Drafts may be written as a sight draft requiring full payment on receipt or as a time draft which allows the buyer to defer payment for a designated period.

2. Letters of credit

Letters of credit are more complex but offer greater protection to both buyer and seller. For this reason it is the most commonly-used method of payment. Essentially, the letter of credit is a bank's guarantee to a buyer that the bank will pay the seller only when certain documents have been delivered to the bank by a specified date. The process works this way: (1) The importer and exporter arrange a sale with an agreement that payment will be made by letter of credit. (2) The importer (buyer) asks a bank to open a letter of credit in favor of the exporter, describing the documents required and conditions to be met prior to payment. (3) The bank issues the letter of credit and sends it to a correspondent bank near the exporter. (4) That bank gives a copy to the exporter. (5) The exporter arranges for shipping and prepares the specified documents. (6) The exporter turns over all specified documents to the second bank, which then pays the exporter. (7) The documents are forwarded to the first bank for reimbursement. (8) The first bank collects payment from the importer and turns over all documents. (9) Those documents allow the importer to pick up the shipment from the carrier. **Caution:** Make sure the letter has been confirmed by your American bank before commencing step (5).

3. Open account sales

Open account sales require no documents, cost the least, and are the simplest method of dealing with buyers. While these are very common in the U.S., they are only used in international trade when the buyer has a well-established business reputation and the seller has gained considerable trust through a long, successful relationship.

4. Export sales insurance

Even with careful sales negotiations, detailed credit checks, and the use of the methods of payment we have looked at, unexpected events may cause losses in international sales. To project against this, export sales insurance is available through the Foreign Credit Insurance Association (FCIA), which operates in partnership with the Export-Import Bank, an independent agency of the U.S. government. Policies are available to cover all of an exporter's credit sales or for a one-time transaction. A special small business policy is available for firms averaging less than $200,000 per year in export sales. Arrangements can be made through your international bank.

c. IMPORTING

Much of what I described under exporting applies equally well to importing. Only now, you're the buyer instead of the seller; so there are different things to be concerned with. For instance, just as an exporter has a choice of direct or indirect selling, the importer has a choice of direct or indirect purchasing.

Who will you deal with in indirect purchasing? Well, first there are import merchants. These firms buy on their own accounts, stock their own goods, and sell directly to manufacturers, wholesalers, and retailers. Second, there are import commission houses. These firms usually act for an overseas exporter, selling goods on a commission basis from the exporter. A third type of buyer is the resident agent. This is a salesperson usually employed by an overseas firm who solicits sales from wholesalers, jobbers, and retailers within an assigned territory. Fourth is the import broker. This person acts primarily as an intermediary between the buyer and seller. As a buyer, you could tell the broker what your requirements are. He, in turn, would obtain prices from appropriate sellers overseas. The actual sale would be handled as a direct transaction between the buyer and overseas seller. Finally, there are wholesalers whose main business is domestic products, but who engage in some importing. They purchase goods for their own stock from various sources for resale to retailers here.

Direct purchasing involves dealing directly with one or more of the following:

(a) A foreign manufacturer or producer
(b) A foreign export merchant — a middleman for foreign manufacturers — who is experienced in the mechanics of exporting where the manufacturers may not be
(c) A foreign broker, similar to the import broker in function, with the main difference being his nearness to foreign sources of supply
(d) A foreign commissionaire (a person who acts as a purchasing agent for you by actually buying goods and shipping them to you for a commission)
(e) An American travelling buyer, usually an employee specializing in the purchase of certain types of goods

(f) Foreign trade fairs and occasional fairs conducted in this country by foreign companies or countries

All goods brought into the country are subject to duty unless there is a specific exemption. Duties may be either "ad valorem", which is a percentage applied to the value, "specific", which is a set amount per unit of measure, or "compound" — a combination of both. Duties on every conceivable product are published annually in the *Tariff Schedule of the United States*. Often a product can easily be classified into several different categories. Where the rate is critical to maintaining a competitive price, it is wise to obtain a written decision from the U.S. Customs Service.

Any shipment into the country valued over $500 must have a special customs invoice. This Form 5515 is available from U.S. consular offices throughout the world. A separate commercial invoice is required, giving all data to determine appropriate duty.

Every foreign article entering the country must be marked with the English name of the country of origin, unless a specific exemption has been provided.

Importers must be aware and up to date on what goods are restricted or prohibited. Currently these include the following:

(a) Obscene, immoral, and seditious matter (to protect our local pornographers, I guess)

(b) Narcotic drugs and derivatives, with certain exceptions under special permit

(c) Alcoholic beverages and confectionary, except under special permit from the Alcohol, Tobacco, and Firearms Division, Internal Revenue Service, Washington, D.C. 20224

(d) Arms, ammunition, and implements of war, except under special license — again from the Alcohol, Tobacco, and Firearms Division

(e) Counterfeit coins, currency, stamps, and securities

(f) Gold and silver coins and articles, under special regulations by the Department of Treasury

(g) Unlicensed imports from designated counties like China, Cuba, Vietnam, etc.

(h) Articles bearing names or marks copying or simulating trademarks, trade names, and copyrights of American firms — except with written consent

(i) Foods, drugs, devices, hazardous substances, and cosmetics under regulations of the Food and Drug Administration, Department of Health, Education, and Welfare, Washington, D.C. 20204

(j) Wool, fur, textile, and fabric products under labelling regulations of the Federal Trade Commision

(k) Wild game animals, birds, fish, reptiles, and parts or products under special regulations of the Bureau of Sports Fisheries and Wildlife, Department of the Interior

(l) Dogs, cats, monkeys, birds, and other pets subject to the quarantine regulations of the Foreign Quarantine Program, National Communicable Disease Center, Atlanta, Ga 30330

(m) Milk and cream, except under permit from the Public Health Service

(n) Livestock, meat, and meat products under regulations of the Department of Agriculture

(o) Fruits, vegetables, plants and plant products, insects, and insecticides under regulations of the Department of Agriculture

(p) Products of convict or forced labor

(q) Nuclear reactors and radioactive material under regulations

(r) Other miscellaneous items like switch blade knives and goods found to be in unfair competition.

One thing that importers must keep in mind in pricing imported goods is the Anti-Dumping Act. Imports must not be sold to American purchasers at less than fair value. Violators are subject to assessment of special dumping duties by the U.S. Tariff Commission. For more details on this act refer to Chapter 33 of *Exporting to the United States*. This is available from the Superintendent of Documents, Washington, D.C.

16
MANAGING EMPLOYEES

No one who has ever run a business questions the value of getting and keeping good employees. Much has been written on the subject. Theories abound but conclusive answers are scarce. There are as many examples of companies that are successful with the "theory X" technique (authoritative management) as of those who are successful with "theory Y" (participative management). There are also, in each case, as many failures. I am going to stay out of that controversy. You must operate in your own way, using your own style. This chapter is going to stress those things that will work, whether you are a tough boss or a persuasive one.

Selecting people is your toughest job. 90% of your mistakes will be people mistakes, not business errors.

There are many techniques for finding, interviewing, and selecting the best possible candidate for a job. You may be interviewing people you've worked with in the past, people recommended to you by friends or associates, people responding to your ad in a local newspaper, referrals from the state employment service or private employment agencies, or just plain walk-ins off the street.

Somewhere out there in the world is a man (or woman) who will be the perfect fit for that job opening in your business. Can you flush out that person? Probably not. There are too many obstacles. The number of people, their wide geographic distribution, and the probability that the right person will not be interested, all work against you in the search. Moreover, it is unlikely that you would recognize that person at first meeting. Signs of nervousness or a displeasing personality might discourage you from the start.

What you will do is pick someone who sells him or herself at the interview, provided that you are satisfied with the background and references presented. You will, no doubt, pick someone you like, but if they prove to be unsuitable later, firing becomes difficult. This is a dilemma we all face.

Once you've made your choice, don't worry about it. It's been my experience that most employees sincerely want to do a good job. Your task then is to guide that natural inclination into produtive channels and be prepared to make the tough decision, if it becomes necessary, to remove an employee who isn't working out. So how do you make a good employee?

a. MOTIVATE

Volumes have been written on motivation. There are many theories on behavior, some very astute and all with some element of truth. This is intended to be a practical book, however, and it is a fact that most small business people have neither the time nor the inclination to shape their companies to suit their employees' heirarchy of needs.

So I am going to home in on four simple points:
- Build pride
- Be consistent
- Listen and communicate
- Cull marginal performers

1. Pride

You know about pride. It is what coaches strive for. It makes winners out of losers. Your employees must have it if their work is to be good.

Your product is the source of your employees' pride, but it is not enough just to have a good product. Your employees must know it is good and must feel that they have contributed to it. The way to get this across is through praise — not only your praise for a job well done but the customer's praise for a fine product.

Get the word around. Ask your customers to say something to your employees when they are in your shop. Show people how their work contributes to the whole.

2. Be consistent

Unless you have turned them off, your employees will try to please you. If you are consistent they will know what you want. When you set goals you must measure progress according to those goals. If you set standards you must insist they be met. If you can force yourself to be consistent you will make it easy to work for you, even though your standards are high.

The best time to start is when you hire someone. Before you make an offer, set out what that person must do and the rules that he or she must follow. This should be written down. Even small companies can prepare personnel manuals. If an employee knows what to expect, he or she will not resent what might otherwise appear to be demeaning.

A large Los Angeles restaurant has a separate locker room with an outside entrance for employees. They must deposit bags and purses in their lockers before entering the restaurant. Nothing can be taken from the restaurant, not even table scraps for dogs. There is no exception to this rule. Employees accept it because it is written in the personnel manual and was made known before they were hired. Had it been imposed after hiring, the employees would have taken it as a slur. Although theft is a major cause for dismissal in the restaurant business, this firm has a low turnover.

If you want to curb personal phone calls, absenteeism, smoking, horseplay, hanky-panky between employees, accepting gratuities, etc., make your rules known in the hiring process.

Actions are more important than words. If you promote people who agree with you, you will have a business full of yes-men. If you treat poor workmanship as natural and unavoidable, you will have a poor quality product. If you accept excuses, you will get them. Your employees will give you what your actions say you want.

As president of the company you want profit and perhaps growth. That is all. Do not get caught in the trap of counting secondary objectives. If you count shipments only, quality will suffer. If you call for cost reductions, shipments can suffer. Your people will score according to your rules.

Bill Russell probably was the most effective basketball player of all time, yet he was not a high scorer. He just won games. When Wilf Chamberlain started playing like Russell, his scores went down but his teams won more games. Your people must know that profits are what you want, not efficient departments. They must cooperate to meet the team goal and some departments must spend effort bolstering others.

3. Listen and communicate

Communication is a two-way deal. Whether you are a manager who hands down decisions from the top or are one who builds from the roots, what matters most is whether your people listen to one another. You must build an atmosphere where people feel free to talk up and know they will be heard. If you do this, the company will have communications.

Every question deserves an answer, and every suggestion should be received with gratitude. People who ask questions and make suggestions are trying to help, even if their motives are self-serving. If allowed to develop, this becomes a source of added power.

4. What about the employee who does not fit?

The most common managerial error is retaining people who cannot do their jobs. Large companies go to the extreme of institutionalizing this mistake, by moving the square pegs around to see whether there are holes they will fit.

A small business absolutely cannot afford this luxury. If you have such a person, take a deep breath and tell him or her goodbye. The sooner the better, for both of you.

One final word on this. Never hang on to a person because he or she appears to be essential. You cannot afford to have such an employee or such a business. If you do, sell it to that person and start something else.

b. COMPENSATION

Relative compensation is more important than actual remuneration, provided the wages you pay are adequate and reasonably competitive. Your salespeople may be making 50% less than the national average and be perfectly happy, but let them discover that the production manager makes $2,000 a year more and all hell breaks loose.

Good young people are never satisfied with their rate of pay for very long, regardless of the circumstances. So you have to keep things in balance and you have to give periodic increases. Still, everyone will not be happy. It is a juggling act without a handy set of instructions. Sorry about that.

c. HANDLING CREATIVE PEOPLE

Employee relations is your toughest job, and handling creative people the toughest part of it. If you are concerned that you have not been able to solve this problem, concern yourself no more. You will always have it and there is no permanent solution, only a series of day-to-day temporizings. A large majority of the highly creative individuals who make up fields of fashion, entertainment, and advertising, and even a large portion of research scientists have personalities that cannot be placated for very long.

What creative employees mean to you

You put up with creative people for one reason: they make your product superior. If you are in such a situation you probably recognize this fact and are willing to go out of your way to satisfy these people. Unfortunately, they have a way of destroying the morale of your other employees. There are times when you must choose between keeping a valuable and talented individual and keeping the rest of your organization. Try to avoid this kind of show down at all costs.

Some broad humor with a touch of deference is a device that has worked well for several managers I have observed.

"Hey, do you think our mathematical genius can fill out a time card?" is a better approach than a straight request. If the rest of the company goes along with the gag, there is an all-around slacking off of tension. Unfortunately, some talented people are too sensitive to be joshed so this technique has its limitations.

17
MORE SUCCESS TIPS

a. REVIEW YOUR MONEY GOAL

Suppose you want to earn, in your own business, $300 per week or $15,000 annually. This is not a large sum of money, nor is wanting to earn that amount per year a pipe dream. Actually, it is a rather modest goal for a business person. But it is a practical one, especially for the first two or three years that you are in business for yourself. If you've been working all your life for someone else, then you most probably have had to get by on an equal amount, or even less, per year.

By setting your financial goal, for the first one or two years of business operation, at $300 weekly, you give yourself a goal that should be easily within your reach, once you know the patterns of success that you must follow in running your own business.

In other words, set your financial goal at the outset, and stay with it, keeping the amount of money you want to earn fixed clearly in your mind's eye. You must, in order to be a successful businessperson, set yourself a goal that is practical, fits in with your life needs, suits your special skills, and above all, fires up your imagination, zeal, and enthusiasm.

b. NEVER STOP LEARNING

The professional businessperson is always experimenting with new ideas. You cannot stand still; you must forge ahead in line with your financial goal. Ideas are part and parcel of progress. True, you will have many ideas that are unworkable, or just not suited to your business needs, but it is extremely important to make a habit of trying to dream up new ways and means of increasing your business profits because, as a "professional," you ought to be in business to make money. Making money should be your prime objective; otherwise, why waste your time, money and efforts?

1. Using your public library

Your local public library is a storehouse of free knowledge, money-making facts, and ideas that you should use. If you ever get a chance to stop in at the public library of any large city, browse through the business and technology sections. You'll be amazed at the wide variety of information available there. Don't forget the state library in Salem. Take a look at all the state and federal statistical reports. You've helped pay for them; try to make some good use of them.

2. How to read books

Most people read books for entertainment but, as a businessperson anxious to learn ways and means of saving money and making more money, you should read books with a dual purpose in mind: for entertainment first, and then, read them again for profit.

I would suggest that you get in the habit of underlining passages you want to remember with a colored pen or pencil (if they are your own books). This is a fast way of pegging down special information that you may need at a later date. That is why building your own library of self-help books is so important to you; you must underline and mark areas in each book that provide you with money-making ideas. If you underline parts of a library book, you're in trouble. So, build a business library of your own. It will pay off in ideas and dollars!

c. YOUR COMPETITION CAN HELP

How can this be, you ask? Other than providing you with a little extra incentive to work harder, you will find, as you progress in running your own business, that opportunities for increasing your profits (doing more in less time) are all around you. Now and then, take time out to look around you to see how your competition is doing, and to see how other people in businesses not linked to your industry, operate. You may learn something that can increase your profits. Profitable ideas are not restricted to any one kind of business. What works well for someone else may work even better for you, provided that you take the idea or method, twist it around, and bend it until it fits in with your needs.

Your competitors have probably instituted some innovation which you never thought of and vice-versa. Talk to them in a frank manner and you will be surprised at the results. You can pick each other's brains in order to make both of you stronger. Don't be afraid that the competition will steal your business. After all, this country is growing fast enough to accommodate all sorts of new businesses. Let's face it. You probably can't expand fast enough even to take care of the natural growth in population. In other words, there's plenty of room for both you and your competitor.

d. MAKE YOUR OWN DECISIONS

It is your life, your business, your future. Get all the help you need from so-called financial experts, accountants, lawyers and bankers, but make all your own decisions. You should always know more about your business than anyone else. This is most important, because other people don't know or care as much about your business as you do. So you must, for your future's sake, always make your own decisions.

Sometimes large fees are paid unnecessarily to so-called "experts" who don't know any more than you do about your business, and often do not know one-eighth as much!

An outside expert whom you call in will not be as concerned over your business problems as you are, despite obvious knowledge or apparent concern. The outsider is usually much more interested in his/her own business affairs than in yours.

When you know as much as your accountant, you can always check and double-check to make sure that what is done is right for you. Be wary of hiring someone who is an "expert." Check credentials before you sign any agreement. In fact, one of the best ways to ensure performance is to base the rate of pay on performance, though this is often easier said than done when dealing with experts.

e. USE TIME EFFECTIVELY

The most important asset you have in business is time — time used to the best possible advantage; time used to plan; time used to think; time used to act! Money you can always manage to get. But time, once lost, can never be recaptured!

The next most important asset you have in business is how you use time to keep on target and achieve your life's goal! Most people waste more time needlessly fighting fear than they use in making money!

Never get into the trap of taking time off from your normal occupation, in which you might have made $20 or $30 for each hour, just to do some menial task that you could pay someone else $5 or $10 an hour to do.

f. ESTABLISH A WORK SCHEDULE

The first and most important step to take is to plan a work schedule — a certain number of hours each day that you must devote to realizing your money goal. If you operate at home, this doesn't mean a working day based on the old nine-to-five grind. Pick the hours best suited to your temperament. But work the number of hours you have to. Don't put it off. If you plan to work nine hours each day, then work your nine hours — not seven or six!

If you choose a certain work schedule, stay with it. Make it a daily habit to put in those work hours, starting the same time each day, and soon it will be second nature to you.

To help you stick to your schedule, make a habit of writing down a list of important things you must do each day and then, as you complete each task, cross it off your list. Don't stop working until every chore on that day's work list has been done! By doing this you will be able to start each new day without any chores left over from the day before.

As you know, work has a bad habit of piling up, and you must accomplish each day's tasks on that day, or else soon your work load will be greater than you can handle. If that happens, you are in trouble!

g. PLAN LEISURE TIME

Up to this point, all we have talked about is work and rightly so, because you must work hard, especially in the early stages, to get your business operating on a sound, money-making basis. But, you know the old saw about "all work and no play." Nobody can work six or seven days a week forever without suffering ill effects, and if your health goes, so does your business!

You should have planned rest periods in which to enjoy your family and friends, rekindle your ambition, and build a new fire under your enthusiasm. Also, and this is important, if you work seven days a week forever, how will you find the time to live and enjoy all the money you make? I don't think it is your intention to work until you drop and then let some relative have a good time on your hard-earned money.

h. KEEP EXPENSES DOWN

This is especially true when getting started. When making purchases, always secure at least three estimates. Never accept the first price offered. Shop around. Better still, try to develop a string of low-cost suppliers. This can be done, no matter how humble your purchasing power. Furthermore, never stop soliciting competitive quotes, even after your business is operating successfully. You will be amazed at how you can lower your costs if you are persistent in this regard.

Your business is your life and your future, so you must wrap your life around your business and be willing to do anything honst to advance yourself. Doing things yourself cuts costs, helps you to know everything that's happening to your business, and gets the job done on time better, usually, than a hired hand would do it! Remember, when you do things yourself, especially early in your ownership career, you are learning, gaining experience, saving money, and paving the way to a secure financial future.

Some people hate minor details. They feel that success is dependent upon only big decisions and big, fancy moves. How untrue! It's how you handle the small things in business that will determine the length and size of your success.

So, the lesson here is that you are not some big-time executive who has a thousand gnomes about to take care of all the little details. You must pay attention to every detail, at least at the start, to ensure success. Do not hire help until you are so overwhelmed with orders that hiring a person will actually *make* you money, not cost you money.

i. IF YOU WANT SOMETHING — ASK FOR IT

Many people are afraid to ask when they need help, or a service, or even when they want to buy something! People can't read your mind, so speak up. Ask for what you want. Moreover, if you ask for a favor, you may be pleasantly surprised. Most people, even hard-nosed businesspeople, like to be asked a favor now and then. It makes them feel needed. Laugh if you like, but this is a fact! Ask a person a favor and you've made a friend.

If you don't ask for anything, how can anyone say yes? Make asking for what you want a habit in your business life.

j. MAKE FREINDS WITH PEOPLE LIKE YOURSELF

Now that you are in business for yourself, running your own business, you will, naturally, have to take a certain amount of time off — to refresh yourself, your outlook, and to re-affirm your determination to reach your money goal. Like everyone else, you will have friends, hobbies, and recreational pleasures in order to help make life worth living. Here's a suggestion that many sound rather mercenary until you realize the full implications of what I mean. Then you'll see the logical money-making merit in this suggestion, and here it is: spend your leisure moments with people who have the same interests in life as you, with people who can help you.

This may sound silly, even boring, but it isn't. It's what all the big-time financial operators do. They mix only with people who can help them, people who have identical business aims — to make money! You can really make your pile of money in a shorter period of time by spending your time off with people who are in a position to help you! Enjoying your leisure time with those who have the same problems, identical business aims, and expert business knowledge as you, will undoubtedly rekindle your ambition and your determination to win.

Another professional aim should be to cultivate the right people — associates who talk the same language as you do. By doing so you'll have more fun, great conversation and, best of all, you'll have countless friends who admire you and wish you success. Why? Because they know full well that, indirectly, your success is their success. How can this be? Well, think it over. By mixing with people who have the same aims in life as you do, you will give them ideas and they, in turn, will give you ideas — like how to get a fast expansion loan, or who may be interested in acting as your local agent for a new product you are putting on the market.

In other words, birds of a feather flock together — usually for mutual protection, advancement and better living. Start now to mix with people who can help you, and you'll be glad you did!

k. GET FREE ADVERTISING THROUGH NEWS RELEASES

Almost any product, service, or professional skill can be pre-sold through using news releases that you write yourself and get printed free in trade papers or newspapers across the country. Also, the new product sections of trade papers and magazines can be a gold mine of free advertising for you. Again, you write and mail news releases using, where advisable, photographs illustrating your product or service. Suitable news releases are printed free — and are a most valuable aid to pre-selling what you have to offer.

So, promote your product or service, at low or no cost, through the medium of the news release, and the new product pages of suitable publications.

Don't let writing the news release frighten you. You don't have to be a professional writer, a copywriter, or a journalist to churn out a suitable news release. It is very simple. You use a standard sheet of white bond paper, size 8-1/2 inches by 11 inches, and you type your release, double-spaced. It is important that you include in your news release only the facts about the product or service you are trying to sell. Usually, the editorial staff of the paper your release goes to will rewrite it to fit it in with their format, anyway.

The facts that should appear in any news release are:

(a) Name, address, and telephone number of your firm
(b) Main selling features of your product or service
(c) What the product will do for the buyer
(d) Price of product or service
(e) How it can be purchased

That's all. Nothing else. If you want to go into a big selling spiel, then you will have to pay for advertising space. The same holds true when you are trying to get free advertising in the new product columns of trade papers. Just be accurate, clear, and short.

1. DOES THE WEATHER AFFECT YOUR BUSINESS

Now, your business may depend a certain amount on the weather. For example, if you operate a marina, then the weather will play an important part in your ultimate success. If your business is presently seasonal, then try to make it a year-round operation. For bigger profits, you must, if possible, turn a seasonal business into a twelve-month profit-making affair. This can be done!

If weather is an important money-making factor in your business, then keep a record of the weather, so that you can make daily and weekly comparisons of how the weather affects your profits. Better still, do some serious thinking, and you may be able to come up with a method of making even the most adverse weather work for you instead of against you. Try it and see what happens.

m. BUSINESS PROTECTION INSURANCE

Businesses, regardless of whether they are retail, wholesale, manufacturing or service-oriented, are all faced with the possibility of burglaries, robberies, shoplifting, employee theft, fire and destruction of property, and customer liability suits. So, businesses must have adequate insurance coverage in order to survive. The two major types of business protection insurance coverage are loss of physical assets and business liability to third parties.

1. Life insurance

Life insurance can also be very important to you, if your family is dependent upon your earnings. This type of life insurance policy provides that, when you die, the disposition of your business will be handled according to your wishes, with the funds being used to finance these wishes. Therefore, business life insurance is one of the best ways to guarantee control and continued value of the business after your death.

2. Partnerships

Many times, partners in a partnership work years to build a successful business. A sudden crisis can develop, should death strike a partner since, by law, the death of one partner immediately dissolves the partnership. The surviving partner's duty under partnership law, unless there is an expressed agreement to the contrary, is to liquidate the business, collect all outstanding accounts, pay off all debts, conserve assets, and account as trustee to the personal representative of the deceased partner for the value of the deceased's interest in the business.

It is possible that, over the years, one partner may accumulate enough assets to buy out the share of the deceased partner. It is true, however, that a buy-sell agreement funded by life insurance on the lives of the partners is the best and most economical way to assure all parties that, on the death of one of them, the transfer of the partnership interest will be carried out smoothly and expeditiously and with the least drain on the decedent's estate and family assets.

In this procedure, each partner applies for a life insurance policy on the life of the other. The applicant is the beneficiary and pays the premiums on his/her partner's life insurance policy. When a partner dies, the funds from the insurance are received by the surviving partner. These funds are then used to purchase the deceased partner's share of the business. The surviving partner retains control of the business, and the heirs of the deceased get cash for their interest.

Similar arrangements may be made to purchase the stock of a deceased shareholder if the business is incorporated.

3. Suppose the "key person" dies?

In most businesses, particularly small ones, there is usually one individual (sometimes more) who makes things go for the business. This person, in many cases, is the president, who actually does most of the work in the business, such as selling, marketing, managing, bookkeeping, and negotiating bank loans. It is the president's imagination, innovations, and ingenuity which contribute largely to the success of the business. If something were to happen to this individual, the business would probably suffer a large financial loss or go out of business.

The company may take out what is called a "key person" life insurance policy on such a person's life. The business is the applicant for the life insurance on the key person's life; it pays the premiums and is the owner and beneficiary. If the key person should die, the cash from the insurance policy can be used to indemnify the company and keep the business in operation, until a replacement is found for the key person. The very fact that the business had the foresight to insure against the hazard of financial loss in case of the death of its key person indicates that the company is serious about its future and has made long-range plans for meeting contingencies. Banks, under these conditions, may be more inclined to give extended consideration for the business's credit requests. The cash from the life insurance on the key person can also be used to keep the business in operation and save the jobs of employees until the business is reorganized or sold.

n. MANAGEMENT COUNSELLING

Most new businesses, at one time or another, could use some management assistance. This is particularly true in small businesses where one or two persons are required to be experts in every aspect of running the business. It's a little like expecting a spouse to be a parent, cook, servant, chauffeur, lover, social secretary, psychiatrist and so on. Sometimes it's just too much and the marriage (business) fails. Before that happens, however, many people wisely look to outside help to pinpoint the problem area and suggest a solution. In addition, because the owners tend to become so involved in day-to-day problems, they lose the overall view, and in these situations, too, an outside consultant can be very useful.

A management counselling service is set up to assist owners and managers of business enterprises, particularly those of smaller enterprises, to improve their methods of doing business and to overcome the problems which confront them.

This counselling service is provided by SCORE (Service Corps of Retired Executives). The talents of these people are provided on a volunteer basis through the Small Business Administration. Their services are particularly worthwhile at a time when you are considering additional financing.

Now the rest is up to you.

Good luck!

READERS PLEASE NOTE: To obtain a free catalog listing other books in the Self-Counsel Press series, please write to:

Self-Counsel Press Inc.
1303 N. Northgate Way
Seattle, Washington 98133

APPENDIX

REFERENCE MATERIAL YOU MAY FIND USEFUL

Business Plan for Small Service Firms
Free from SBA

Business Plan for Small Manufacturers
Free from SBA

Business Plan for Small Construction Firms
Free from SBA

Starting and Managing a Small Business
$1.35 from SBA

Ratio Analysis for Small Business
90¢ from SBA

What is the Best Selling Price?
Free from SBA

Choosing the Legal Structure for Your Firm
Free from SBA

Financial Recordkeeping for Small Stores
$1.30 from SBA

Franchising Opportunities Handbook
$3.10 from Superintendent of Documents
Washington, D.C. 20402

Evaluating Oregon's Tax Option in Pollution Control Facilities, Special Report 316
Free from Oregon State University Extension Service

BIBLIOGRAPHY

Bauchens, John H., *Exporter's Guide*. Olympia, WA: Washington State Department of Commerce & Economic Development, 1973.

Bauchens, John H. *Importer's Guide*. Olympia, WA: Washington State Department of Commerce & Economic Development, 1975.

Broom, N. H., and Longenecker, J. G. *Small Business Management*. 4th ed. Cincinnati: Southwestern Publishing Co., 1975.

Clark, Douglas L. *Start a Successful Business in Washington*. 1st ed. Vancouver, B.C.: Self-Counsel Pres, Inc., 1976.

Commerce Clearing House, Inc. *State Tax Guide*. Chicago: Commerce Clearing House, Inc., 1976.

Commerce Clearing House, Inc. *U.S. Master Tax Guide*. Chicago: Commerce Clearing House, Inc., 1974.

J. K. Lasser Tax Institute. *J. K. Lasser's Business Tax Techniques*. New York: Simon and Schuster, 1967.

J. K. Lasser Tax Institute. *J. K. Lasser's Your Income Tax*. New York: Simon and Schuster, 1975.

Kelly, Ernest S. *Starting a Successul Business in Canada*. 2nd ed. Vancouver, B.C.: Self-Counsel Press, Inc., 1976.

Pickle, H. B., and Abrahamson, R. L. *Small Business Management*. New York: John Wiley and Sons, Inc., 1976.

Oregon Business Workshops Speech Transcripts. *Managing New and Expanding Business in Oregon*. Eugene, Medford, Pendleton: December, 1974.

Oregon Department of Commerce. *Site Selection Data.* Salem, OR: Oregon Department of Commerce, n.d.

Oregon Department of Economic Development. *Doing Business in Oregon.* 6th ed. Salem, OR: Oregon Department of Economic Development, 1975.

Oregon Department of Transportation. *Survey of Oregon Ports, Economic Impact Section, 1972.* Salem, OR: Oregon Department of Transportation, 1973.

Oregon State Highway Division, *1971 Out-of-State Tourist Revenue Study,* Salem, OR: Oregon State Highway Division, 1972.

Meier, Harvey A., comp. *Government Requirements for Filing and Reporting Business Activities: A Manual for New and Existing Oregon Businesses.* 1st ed. Corvallis, OR: Oregon State University Extension Service, 1973.

Walker, Jenepher, ed. *Small Business Reporter.* Vol. 12, no. 6: Exporting. San Francisco: Bank of America, 1974.

U.S. Army Corps of Engineers. *Waterborne Commerce of the United States, 1975.* Part IV. San Francisco [Washington, D.C.: Government Printing Office, 1976 (?)].

U.S. Department of Commerce. Domestic and International Business Administration. *U.S. Industrial Outlook 1976: With Projections to 1985.* Washington, D.C.: Government Printing Office, 1976.

U.S. Department of Commerce. Office of Minority Business Enterprise. *Federal Programs Assisting Minority Enterprise.* Washington, D.C.: Government Printing Office, 1971.

U.S. Department of Defense. Office of Assistant Secretary of Defense Installations and Logistics. *Small Business and Labor Surplus Area Specialists Designated to Assist the Businessman.* Washington, D.C.: Government Printing Office, 1973.